MEETINGS AND
COMMITTEE
PROCEDURE

This book is due for return on or before the last date shown below.

a+ e413

10

MEETINGS AND COMMITTEE PROCEDURE

Gordon R. Wainwright

TEACH YOURSELF BOOKS

Hodder and Stoughton

First published 1987

Copyright © 1987
Gordon R. Wainwright

British Library Cataloguing in Publication Data

Wainwright, Gordon R.
  Meetings and committee procedure.
  1. Meetings
  I. Title
  658.4'563   AS6

  ISBN 0 340 40213 X

*Printed and bound in Great Britain for
Hodder and Stoughton Educational,
a division of Hodder and Stoughton Ltd,
Mill Road, Dunton Green, Sevenoaks, Kent,
by Richard Clay Ltd, Bungay, Suffolk.
Photoset by Rowland Phototypesetting Ltd,
Bury St Edmunds, Suffolk*

Contents

Author's Note

Many of the terms which are traditionally used in the course of meetings are male-oriented. Clearly, the chair can equally well be occupied by a woman, but to address someone as Chairwoman seems cumbersome and to address them as Chair seems vaguely insulting. For this reason, the male pronoun has usually been used in this book. It has been done only for convenience, however, and should not be taken to imply a sexist attitude.

1

Introducing Meetings

The only organisation which can survive without meetings is the genuinely one-man business. And even he will have to attend meetings elsewhere if he is to market his products or services, negotiate agreements and make sales. Meetings are an inescapable facet of life in a modern industrial society.

We find ourselves involved in meetings at every level from the family conference on where to spend this year's summer holiday to the formal annual general meeting of large corporations. They can take many forms: one person interviewing another for a job, a small group meeting to solve a common problem, a large group called together to discuss a pressing local issue, or a committee which meets regularly to consider an organisation's affairs.

A meeting may be defined as a number of people (from two to several thousands) who come to a pre-arranged place at a pre-arranged time to discuss, and usually decide upon, matters of common interest. It may last a few minutes or it may last several hours. It may be informal, in the sense that it follows no set procedural pattern, or it may be formal, in that the rules laid down for its conduct are closely observed.

Clearly, meetings will have many differences. But they will also possess certain common characteristics. It is the purpose of this book to explore both the differences and the similarities and, in so doing, provide a guide to the better management of meetings and committees.

Dissatisfaction with meetings

You might expect that, since meetings are so common and vital to our conduct of our affairs, they would be universally accepted and even welcomed by those who have to take part in them. But this is not so. In fact, dissatisfaction with meetings is so widespread that it is worth considering in more detail. It will give us an indication of some of the reasons why so many people find it difficult to use them effectively. Hence, it will also show why a book like this is necessary in order that more people can discover how to make meetings more productive. If this can be achieved it will help to reduce the dissatisfaction and may even contribute towards creating a situation in which meetings actually become pleasurable and satisfying.

The most common source of dissatisfaction with meetings is that *there are too many of them*. That, at least, is what many people believe and, in a very real sense, if people believe something to be true then, for them, it is true for all practical purposes. Sometimes it even seems that meetings are called to discuss what will happen at another meeting that the people concerned are scheduled to attend. The phenomenon of 'talks about talks' is common in the field of industrial relations, for example, and in the conduct of local government affairs it is common for the political parties to have their own 'group' meetings in advance of committee meetings to decide what their political stance is to be on key items on the agenda.

Meetings last too long. That is a common objection and it is true that many of them keep people away from the other work they have to do, for unacceptable periods of time. There are few things more frustrating than having to sit through the whole of a meeting when your own involvement is restricted to two or three items which concern you directly. It seems to be the case that when a number of people sit round a table, which is the usual setting for a meeting, they appear to be reluctant to depart until everything that could possibly be discussed has been discussed.

Many meetings avoid taking hard and fast decisions if they can. It is inevitable that when several people meet together they will have a variety of opinions and attitudes on the matters to be considered. If, as often happens, there is no clear consensus for a particular course of action, then it is by no means uncommon for a decision to be deferred. This is frequently done on the basis of the excuse that more information is required before a decision can be taken.

Often the wrong people attend meetings. This is common in organisations where the attendance at a meeting is specified according to the position a person occupies, for instance, sales manager or personnel manager. In these circumstances, deputies may be sent along and they may not possess the degree of knowledge or expertise particular agenda items require. In large departments, it may not even be the same person each time who attends a meeting and this further undermines the potential effectiveness of the event.

Meetings are often badly run. The skills of chairmanship are not too difficult to acquire, but many people who find themselves taking the chair at meetings learn to do it by wasteful trial and error methods. There seems to be a reluctance by many of those who attend meetings to learn anything about chairmanship until they actually find themselves in the chair. But by then it is usually too late. Training in any skill needs to begin well before the trainee has to deal with a real-life situation. That is why almost all driving schools teach the fundamental techniques of driving on a special driving area or at least at a place where there is no traffic.

The accusation is frequently made that *meetings are held for the sake of meeting.* Some people can become so addicted to meetings that they do call them for insufficient reasons. Wiser heads will avoid such meetings where they can, but if the boss or the president of your club calls a meeting it can be difficult to decline the invitation. We shall consider in Chapter 11 some of the things that can usefully be done to avoid problems like this arising.

Many people are guilty of inadequate preparation for meetings. They come along and have not properly read the papers and reports which have been sent out in advance, for example. There is no excuse for this. No one should allow themselves to become so inundated with work or other activities that they attend meetings and are, as it were, flying by the seat of their pants. At the very least they should learn something about the techniques of rapid reading, which will show them how to process large amounts of information in less time and with greater productivity.

Having said this, there can be *too much paperwork* associated with certain kinds of meetings. If those who attend meetings have a responsibility to develop more efficient reading techniques, then the converse of this is that those who prepare minutes and reports for meetings have a responsibility to express themselves clearly and concisely. The one cannot really be done effectively without the other.

It must also be remembered that where meetings are held during the working day in an organisation they have a *high cost*. It is not difficult to quantify this by assessing what proportion of the working week has been spent in the meeting. From each person's salary it can then be calculated how much their attendance at a meeting has cost. Multiply that figure by the number of meetings those people attend in a year and you have a figure which should make any organisation pause and consider whether it is using its meetings as efficiently as it might.

For some reason, *many meetings with a pre-arranged starting time begin late*. A lot will depend on how important those attending think the meeting is, but, as was made clear in the previous paragraph, time costs money. When meetings do not begin on time, money is certainly being wasted.

Where they are not properly directed, *meetings wander* from the items they are supposed to be discussing and move into irrelevant areas, or they go over old ground, perhaps because one or two of those present are riding hobby horses about those subjects. Firm but courteous chairmanship is the principal means whereby this can be avoided, but everyone who attends a meeting has a responsibility to see that it keeps to the point.

One of the most frustrating kinds of meetings to have to attend is the *'rubber stamping' meeting* where matters have really been decided in a sub-committee or working party but formality dictates that the parent body has to give its approval. Where it can be achieved, of course, meetings like this should be avoided, if only on cost grounds. Where they cannot, then they should be conducted as briskly as politeness permits.

A good many people who attend meetings where they are the 'junior members' complain of *inadequate opportunities to partici-pate* in the proceedings. We shall consider in Chapter 5 ways in which active participation can be encouraged and achieved. For those who are itching to become more fully involved in the meetings they have to attend, this should be a particularly useful chapter.

Many chairmen, in their search for agreement from a meeting, place such an *emphasis on consensus and compromise* as to undermine the effectiveness of the meetings they conduct. Achieving these ends may be satisfying to chairmen, but it is another source of very real dissatisfaction with those who somehow have to translate the consensus or the compromise into action.

Other chairmen actively encourage conflict between meeting participants in the mistaken belief that conflict in an organisation is healthy. So it can be, where it arises naturally out of differing approaches to the methods of solving problems. There is little purpose in engendering it for the sake of making what might otherwise be a quietly running, efficient organisation appear to be dynamic and bursting with new ideas.

Participants, too, can be guilty of trying to do things for which

Fig. 1 Reasons for dissatisfaction with meetings

Dissatisfaction	**Reason**	**Chapter**
1 There are too many meetings	Poor preparation	3,14
2 Meetings last too long	Poor chairmanship	6
3 Decisions are avoided or deferred	Poor chairmanship	6
4 The wrong people attend	Poor preparation	3
5 Meetings are badly run	Poor chairmanship	6
6 Meetings are held for the sake of meeting	Poor preparation	3,14
7 People have not read the papers beforehand	Poor preparation	3
8 There is too much paperwork	Poor preparation	3
9 Meetings are costly	Poor preparation	2,3
10 Meetings start late	Poor chairmanship	6
11 Meetings wander from the point	Poor chairmanship	6
12 Some meetings simply act as 'rubber stamps'	Poor preparation	3,14
13 Many people do not get the chance to participate in meetings effectively	Poor chairmanship	5,6
14 Consensus and compromise are often sought at the expense of effectiveness	Poor chairmanship	6
15 Conflict may be encouraged	Poor chairmanship	6
16 People have hidden objectives	Poor preparation	2,6

meetings are not necessarily the best battlegrounds. Such actions can often stem from *'hidden objectives'* which people bring with them to meetings and we shall consider how these operate and what should be done about them in the next chapter.

It would be possible to continue for some time listing and exploring the various dissatisfactions which people feel as far as meetings are concerned, but there is a danger in being too negative and it is time we considered the reasons for the dissatisfactions and then move on to what can be done to remedy things and move towards a situation in which more people can be satisfied with meetings than are dissatisfied.

Reasons for dissatisfaction

For the sake of convenience and conciseness, these are listed in Fig. 1. Whilst Chapter 11 is concerned with problems with meetings, other chapters will cover other aspects of activities such as chairmanship and preparation and so a main chapter reference is included which some readers may find helpful if they wish to pursue a particular matter.

Why meetings are important

Despite the dissatisfactions and the frustrations, the fact remains that meetings are important and, in many instances, necessary. They are not a problem which can be solved by removing them from the organisational scene. They possess certain characteristics which we need to recognise and bear in mind as we seek to improve our mastery of the techniques of managing meetings and committees.

Group discussion is a powerful means of persuasion. Stubborn individuals who adopt a position and then refuse to budge from it, even in the face of all the evidence, will be easier to move when they see that most other people have come to a different conclusion from themselves. It takes a very brave, or foolhardy, person to pursue a wayward or maverick course against the pressure that the opposition of a group presents. Pressure groups are aptly named and, indeed, all groups are in a sense pressure groups, because a group will usually have more credibility than an individual. Exceptions abound in history, of course, of individuals who went against their groups and in the end had their positions vindicated, but in everyday affairs a group, properly mobilised and directed, is a powerful force.

Groups, whether in the form of meetings or in less formal discussions and get-togethers, involve people in matters of mutual concern and are a force for the improvement of attitudes. A manager or even a politician who seeks to introduce significant change without first involving those affected in consultation and discussion, is pursuing a rash course indeed in this day and age.

It also has to be borne in mind that people will support decisions much more enthusiastically if they have had a hand in making them. The decisions then become their own rather than the property of a select and perhaps mistrusted few. Once this happens, the sense of involvement and identification which results will help to ensure that courses decided upon will be put into effect rather than run into the sandbanks of apathy and reluctance.

Where groups do not operate effectively there can be serious dangers. There are always dangers when power becomes concentrated in too few hands and this is almost always the consequence of not having active participation through meetings, committees and other forms of group process.

The modern organisation is too complex usually for one person to run it and there is a need for people with different kinds of expertise and knowledge. This means that knowledge is pooled through the use of groups. Continuity of thought and action are better maintained and decisions have the necessary backing. The use of minutes or some other form of recording the proceedings of meetings means that a reliable record exists of decisions and it is possible to monitor progress much more efficiently. The whole process of involving people and doing it on a systematic basis means that their various individual inputs result in output that is truly synergic, in that the outcome is greater in achievement than the mere totalling of the individual inputs would suggest. Groups working as teams can attain what a number of unco-ordinated individuals can never aspire to. Good meetings, then, are an essential component in any attempt to improve the range and quality of communication between people.

Overview of the book

Having set the stage, as it were, it will be useful at this point if we look ahead at what is to come and see how this book will guide you, step by step, towards the better management of meetings and committees. In setting out on any journey into the largely unknown, it is essential to have a map of the terrain so that you can be on the look-out for particular features you are interested in and so that you can more clearly see the general context in which your journey is taking place.

We shall begin our journey in Chapter 2 with the *Purposes and Preconditions* of meetings. The purposes which meetings can satisfy will be considered, together with the need to specify in advance what the main purpose or purposes will be. There will be a preliminary discussion of when an agenda is needed and what kinds of items it should contain. We shall look at factors such as the best sizes for meetings, how to decide who should attend (where there is a choice in the matter), the best locations for meetings, how to estimate how long a meeting is likely to take, how to select a chairman (if one is necessary and where there is a choice) and how to decide the best form for the minutes or the record of the proceedings (again, where there is a choice). We shall also consider the various types of meetings which most of us are likely to encounter either at work or in the course of following a leisure interest.

Chapter 3 deals with *Action Before a Meeting* and will show you how to brief yourself properly and in the minimum necessary time on the agenda items. The assembling of background information which will assist active and productive participation in meetings is also covered. The need to see meetings not in isolation in many cases but as a sequence, and the resultant need to retain an awareness of the things the meeting or committee has dealt with in the past is discussed. There is even a reminder of the often overlooked politeness of apologising for absence if unable to attend a particular meeting.

How a Meeting Proceeds is the subject of Chapter 4 and is concerned with how a group of people ensures, through their various roles (chairman, secretary and participants, for example), that the meeting gets through the business it has to. The specific roles are explored in later chapters, so this one deals with how meetings work through their agendas, what is the best order in which to place items, the main 'rules of debate', how to frame motions or resolutions and amendments (with examples), what points of order are and how they should be used, what a quorum is and why you usually need one, the procedural motions which are used in formal meetings and how a meeting can tell when it has reached a decision.

In Chapter 5, the subject is *How to Participate in a Meeting* and is for those who are in attendance but who do not have a specific role, such as chairman, secretary or treasurer, to fulfil. It will show you how to prepare in advance for any contribution that you think you might want to make. It will tell you how to find out what a committee or other groups have done in the past, the importance of knowing who else will be at a meeting and the desirability of finding out as much about them as possible. It shows you how to use body language in order to get a word in edgeways and then to get your message across effectively. Other topics covered are the importance of participating early in a meeting, how to make notes (with examples), how to overcome objections to your point of view, techniques for making a presentation to a group of people, how to build on areas of common agreement and how practice builds confidence and improves performance.

The Chair is the focus of attention in Chapter 6 and the nature of chairmanship is explained. The importance of a chairman to the success of most meetings is explored and several styles of chairmanship are outlined with an assessment of the most effective. You will learn how to control meetings and vary your style to suit the circumstances. How a chairman should deal with the 'hidden agenda' and techniques for coping with expressions of aggression and other disruptive behaviour are covered here. Techniques for resolving conflict as practised by various types of group are discussed, as is the whole question of the role of conflict in meetings. Other matters explained are techniques for democratising meetings and reducing the role of the chairman so that others can express themselves more fully, how to keep a meeting to the points at issue, how to pace a meeting, how to summarise a discussion and when votes are necessary.

Chapter 7 is concerned with *The Secretary*. Even very informal meetings can benefit by having someone who, in effect, occupies the role of secretary for them and, if the chairman is the most important person during a meeting, the secretary is the most important in all other respects. The chapter will show how the secretary influences the agenda, how he influences the chairman and how, whereas chairmen may come and go, the secretary usually has a much longer 'life span'. The secretary's roles as the group's memory, as link man, and as the group's 'ambassador' are explored. Although the chairman rules on procedure, the secretary may well be the person he looks to for advice, so a secretary needs to know 'the rule book'. How the secretary should brief himself is covered, as well as the tasks to be completed before a meeting takes place, how to think ahead to the writing of the minutes, what the secretary's role is when it comes to a vote, the problems a secretary may face during a meeting and how to deal with them, and how to brush up on the law of meetings where this is necessary.

Chapter 8 is about *Writing the Minutes* or the record of what happened at the meeting. It explains what minutes are (with examples) and what they need to achieve. The need for the accurate recording of decisions is emphasised, as well as the need to record all motions in formal meetings whether they are carried through or not. Minutes should keep to the order of the agenda and a secretary can benefit by planning ahead for this. The tone and style appropriate for minutes is described. The dangers of making minutes too brief or too lengthy are considered and the value of having two people making notes at important meetings so that cross checking can take place is discussed. The need to have minutes in draft form so that the chairman can check them is considered, together with an evaluation of those occasions on which minutes are neither necessary nor desirable.

Action After a Meeting is covered in Chapter 9 because meetings do not exist in isolation. They are but a part of a larger process. This chapter explains the value of having an action sheet for the things that you have to do and for those things that others have to do (with examples). Checking that action has been taken, arranging subsequent meetings, informing others of the group's decisions, checking the minutes, filing, writing memos, letters and reports resulting from the meeting are other topics covered here. The chapter concludes with a consideration of moving into the preparation cycle for the next meeting and emphasises the fact that for many of us meetings are a continuous process.

Chapter 10 deals with *Particular Kinds of Meetings* so that you can see how to apply the techniques of managing meetings and committees to such meetings as formal committees (for example, those of the local council, to many of which the general public now have a right of attendance), informal committees, working parties and discussions, negotiations and industrial relations meetings, club and society meetings, political meetings, trades union meetings, conferences and seminars, company meetings, disciplinary meetings and other business and professional meetings.

Problems with Meetings are considered in Chapter 11 and cover such aspects as meetings which last too long, inability to reach a quorum (where this is necessary), becoming entangled in procedural difficulties, having too many amendments 'on the table' at any one time, too many points of order, weak chairmanship, confusion over what has been decided, disruptive behaviour and other problems already indicated earlier in this chapter.

Chapter 12 is concerned with *Analysing Meetings* because a great deal can be learned about how to improve an activity if the reasons for its failure to be completely effective can be understood. Items on which the analysis is based include assessing the quality of preparation, achievement of objectives, sequence of items, attention given to each item, the actions of the chairman, clarity of decisions, the length of the meeting, the involvement by the chairman of the other people present, the effectiveness of each participant's involvement, clarity of action after the meeting, and the drawing of conclusions from the analysis and acting upon them.

Chapter 13 deals with the important subject of *Preparing and Presenting Reports to Meetings*. You will learn a five-step strategy for speedy, effective report writing which covers preparation, assessment, planning, expression and review. The techniques of effective report presentation are explained, including the desirability of not reading the report aloud but working from notes, drawing attention to key features and answering questions clearly and concisely. Accuracy, conciseness, clarity and simplicity are emphasised as basic rules. The need for sensitivity to your own and others' body language when you are presenting a report is discussed, as well as the need to concentrate on the evidence and rational argument, making sure you can be heard and using visual aids to improve the impact of a presentation.

In Chapter 14 we explore *Alternatives to Meetings* such as delegation of some activities to named individuals who may report back to the group at intervals rather than continually, using telephone calls to test opinion, using the 'nil return' concept when there are no problems arising, feeding information in to a central memory to which everyone has access where computer work stations are available and periodically reviewing the meetings and committee structure to eliminate those which have served their purpose and are no longer required.

The Treasurer or financial adviser and other officers are considered in Chapter 15. Not every organisation will require a treasurer, but for those which do some guidelines are offered to assist the person appointed to serve the group as best he can and for the group to obtain the maximum value from having such expertise available to it. The roles of a vice-chairman and of various other officers are also discussed.

Committee Language is explained in Chapter 16 for those who are not yet familiar with terms such as rules of debate, standing orders, quorum, agenda, amendments, rescinding resolutions, ad hoc committees, points of order, extraordinary meetings, ex-officio members of committees and many others which are likely to be encountered in a variety of contexts. It is a reference chapter to which you should feel free to refer any time you encounter an unfamiliar term.

Chapter 17 offers a *Checklist for Effective Meetings* which should help you to ensure that nothing of importance has been overlooked before, during or after a meeting.

The book concludes with a list of Further Reading for those who wish to explore the subject of managing meetings and committees, or some particular aspect of it, in more detail. There is also an index which should assist in locating topics which have not been included in this general overview.

2

Purposes and Preconditions

Despite the general importance and frequent inevitability of meetings and because of the dissatisfactions many people express about meetings, the first question we have to ask ourselves is: *Is a meeting really necessary?*

There really is no point in our proceeding further if in our heart of hearts we know that there is a better way of dealing with things than by means of a meeting. If, as you read this, you are in fact at the point at which you have to decide whether or not to call a meeting, you might even like to glance ahead to Chapter 14, on Alternatives to Meetings.

However, let us suppose that the answer to the question is 'Yes'. The next step we have to take is to determine the purpose of the meeting.

Purposes of meetings

In a sense, there can be almost as many purposes in holding a meeting as there are meetings, because each meeting will be unique and, in some way or other, will deal with matters no other meeting has ever dealt with. If you find yourself in a meeting which is simply covering ground already covered elsewhere, you really are wasting your time and should do something about it. In that sense, each meeting you attend is a creative experience because something somewhere within its confines must be original. It is a thought that might provide a crumb of comfort in a meeting which seems to be rambling interminably around a well-worn theme.

In the main, however, the purposes of meetings are of about a dozen different kinds.

A meeting may be called to *co-ordinate activities*. That is to say, it may be necessary on a regular basis to bring certain people together so that each can report what he has been doing and so that any possibly wasteful overlapping of activities can be avoided. It is difficult, if not impossible, for this to be achieved other than through the mechanism of a meeting. Certainly, people seem to express less dissatisfaction with this kind of meeting than they do with many others. If people can see a clear purpose to a meeting they are bound to be happier, especially if they can see some clear benefit to themselves and this is usually the case with co-ordination meetings. Everyone can emerge with a better picture not only of the contribution they are making to the enterprise, whatever it is, but also of the relative contributions of others. It helps people to feel they are part of a team.

A meeting may be called to *build morale*. This may not be the explicitly stated purpose. Indeed, if it is, it almost certainly will not work, but it may be what the convenor of the meeting really has in mind. A co-ordination meeting can, in fact, very well be used for this purpose as well. Morale is promoted when people can identify with whatever a group is seeking to achieve. Again, if the meeting can help people to feel that they are part of a team, they will usually regard this as a worthwhile end and participate willingly.

A meeting may be called in order to *provide a framework within which risks can be shared* where difficult decisions have to be made. Those who are affected by such decisions will tend to find them more palatable if they can see that they have been arrived at after due consideration. It is another example of the power and strength of the group which we looked at in the last chapter.

A manager or leader will need to call his subordinates together from time to time in order to *brief them on the current state of the organisation's affairs*, or in new safety procedures, or methods of working, or for staff training purposes, or for any one of a multitude of other reasons. If the purpose is clearly identified and communicated to those who have to attend, it will make the resultant meeting much more productive.

Problem-solving is a purpose for which meetings are very commonly called. If the approach is a creative one, such meetings can be immensely beneficial to an organisation. It is foolish for an individual to struggle with a problem if several minds can be brought to bear upon it. The old adage that two heads are better than one can be extended to enable us to say that several heads are even better.

If a manager has a decision of some importance to make, even if it is not a particularly controversial one, it can be useful to *call people together and consult them* on it. This seems to be something which those managers who believe that 'management must manage' are reluctant to do. It is a pity to take such a narrow view of the role of the manager because, whatever the outcome, once again most people appreciate being involved even when they are not actually instrumental in affecting the nature of the decision that is ultimately made.

Meetings may simply be called to *exchange information*. Such meetings need not be long. Indeed, they may even be taken standing up. This is a simple but very effective technique for ensuring that meetings do not last longer than is necessary to serve their purpose.

Meetings may be called to *make policy for an organisation*. Such meetings will usually be among the more lengthy ones because there will be many factors to consider and it is worth taking time over this kind of activity because of the wider effects that policies inevitably have over day-to-day activities. Get the policy right and properly spelled out and there should be much less trouble with the details of its implementation. It is only when people are really in the dark over what they have to do that mistakes occur and grievances develop.

Indeed, the *expression of grievances* and the *letting-off of steam* are other purposes for which meetings may be called. Often such meetings are avoided, in the misguided view that if you ignore trouble it will sooner or later go away. It is much better to grasp the nettle and bring dissatisfactions out into the open. Leave them to fester and they will at some time in the future burst forth as much more serious and fundamental problems. An organisation which can openly and freely discuss its sources of internal irritation has a much better chance of surviving as an organisation than one which seeks to regard those with dissident points of view as 'trouble makers' and will not discuss grievances until it has to and then only reluctantly.

Meetings may be called to *persuade people* to a point of view or to agree with a set of proposals. As such, they are essential to the processes of democracy. By definition, unless you are in the Mafia, you cannot persuade people unless you can convince them that they should change!

Or a meeting may simply be called to *explore an issue* without prior commitment to action on anyone's part. Such meetings can be very frustrating unless there is some kind of tacit agreement on the part of those involved to limit the time the meeting will take. Otherwise the meeting may ramble on for a long time and get nowhere.

In addition to these and other possible purposes, individuals may have other 'hidden objectives' in calling or attending meetings. For the sake of increasing the effectiveness of meetings and committees, you should avoid having hidden objectives as far as possible, but since you need to be able to recognise them in others they are listed in Fig. 2. You may well be able to add to the list from your own experience.

Fig. 2   Hidden objectives

Quite apart from all the legitimate purposes for which a meeting may be called or for which a person may attend a meeting, there are 'hidden' objectives to be watched for.

A person may call or attend a meeting in order to:

1   impress others who have not been invited to attend;
2   discredit a rival, especially if the rival is not present;
3   show superiority, perhaps through having a special report on the agenda;
4   work out his or her frustrations or problems on the other people attending the meeting;
5   gain promotion by turning in a good performance which will attract the attention of superiors;
6   build an empire by having other people reporting in to him or her;
7   make life difficult for others in some way, possibly by calling the meeting at an inconvenient time;
8   defend his or her 'territory' by making it seem more important;
9   make life easier for himself or herself, possibly by allocating tasks to others at the meeting;
10 ride a hobby horse which appears somewhere on the agenda.

Preliminary consideration of the agenda

We shall deal in detail with the construction of an agenda for a meeting in Chapter 7, but it is useful even at a very early stage in the run-up to a meeting to give some thought to the kind of items it should contain. It is even worth asking yourself whether an agenda is necessary. As a general rule, very informal meetings will have no agenda as such, although the participants may nevertheless have a number of subjects in mind which they wish to discuss.

An agenda is needed if there is to be any degree of formality (in the sense of following set rules of procedure) in the meeting, or if there are items on which people will need to brief themselves in advance or on which they are to be given reports or other documents to study. As an approximate guide, an agenda which contains more than about a dozen items probably indicates that a group is not meeting frequently enough to deal with its business or it is trying to do too much at once and should set up a subcommittee to deal with minor matters or matters requiring detailed and lengthy scrutiny.

Many meetings will have certain regular items to cover, such as the minutes of the last meeting, matters arising from the minutes, secretary's report, treasurer's report, reports from sub-committees and any other business. In addition, there will be items on which there are special reports. There should be as few of these as possible, for a meeting which tries to deal with more than one or two major items is in real danger of over-running the time which might reasonably be allocated for it.

In addition, there may be items carried over from a previous meeting and in this case these should be placed early in the proceedings and a more careful assessment made of how many new items can be included. People can only give their attention to a limited number of things at any one time, so there could be circumstances when an extra meeting needs to be called. It is as well to be aware of this possibility as soon as is practicable.

Another consideration to bear in mind is whether or not any of the papers for the meeting are unlikely to be ready sufficiently far in advance of the meeting for participants to have a proper chance to study them. Meetings at which papers are circulated at the beginning of the meeting make life very difficult for all concerned. As we shall see in Chapter 7, the secretary and the chairman should get together in advance to make sure that everything will be ready in good time. Others who have reports to feed in to the process also need to bear these points in mind.

Size of meetings

It is not usually possible to have meetings of less than two people, but if they are to be attended by more than about fifteen they will become progressively harder to control or more formal. Formality is, in fact, essential for large numbers for, unless people are prepared to follow quite strict rules (for example, that only one person speaks at a time), a meeting can quickly degenerate into chaos.

So meetings which are too small (say, fewer than four) or too large (say, more than fifteen) should be avoided. In certain circumstances it will be impossible to follow this advice, but it should be borne in mind that research has shown that meetings of between five and nine people are the most desirable for many purposes. Such a size gives everyone the chance to participate fully and people have reported that they gain the greatest satisfaction from meetings of this size. As size increases, participant satisfaction drops and there is also a tendency for large groups to split into sub-groups or factions which has a disruptive effect. It is also worth remembering that as the size of meetings in organisations increases, so do the costs (see Chapter 1).

Attendance of meetings

Very often there is no choice to be exercised over who will attend. The names are determined by position in the organisation or by some other factor. But where choice can be exercised it is worth following some basic principles which will contribute to the effectiveness of a meeting.

Only people who must have an input to the agenda items should be invited. Someone who is only concerned with one item should be expected to stay for that item only. Limit the number of regular attenders to those without whom the meeting cannot put its decisions into effect. Avoid people attending for the sake of attending.

Clearly, there will be many occasions when these principles have to be over-ridden because of courtesy, expediency or other reasons, but the nearer one can approach to observing them the better.

Meeting places

The location or venue at which a meeting will be held will have an effect on the proceedings quite out of proportion to its apparent importance. If the room is too large or too small, too hot or too cold, too draughty, or too high even (that is, in terms of the height of the ceiling), a meeting will be much less effective than it might be. Unless the setting is appropriate, the behaviour of participants will be adversely affected in all manner of small ways. Once again some general principles can be laid down.

The room should be of an appropriate size. Rooms which are too small should be avoided as much as rooms which are too large. It should be comfortable, but not too comfortable. There is little point in bringing together what is essentially a working group of people and then placing them in an environment which is more suited to relaxation. At a practical level, we do not wish to encourage people to doze off. If they do that, they might just as well not be there in the first place. Make sure interruptions will be avoided as far as possible (for example, by not having a telephone in the room). Many organisational meetings may find it useful to have ready access (though perhaps not in the room itself) to a photocopier in case items need to be circulated without notice. As we have said, it is best not to do this, but if it has to be done it is best done quickly. The place of meeting should be as accessible as possible. Rooms up flights of back stairs or at the end of winding corridors should be avoided. There should be sufficient seats for everyone. It may be necessary to have a reserve supply if the numbers attending cannot be accurately predicted in advance. Whether or not to provide ashtrays is another consideration, though a less important one than it once was. It may also be worth providing some form of refreshment. Many people seem to be able to think better if they have had a cup of coffee or tea.

Time for meeting

It is difficult to estimate the length of time a meeting is likely to take, but experience will provide some sort of guide. Usually, it takes about five to ten minutes per item in a reasonably smooth-running business meeting, though it can vary from a couple of minutes to over an hour. Working on an average of ten minutes per item should be generous enough.

A meeting length of about an hour will enable most groups to deal with an acceptable amount of business. In this respect, the chairman has the major role to play, so we shall return to this topic in Chapter 6. The secretary can also assist by introducing items in a way that focuses attention on the decision which has to be made, rather than on less important aspects of the subjects.

Other preliminaries

Where a group has not identified a chairman in advance, it is worth following certain basic principles. A chairman should be a strong enough personality to maintain order. One does not want a little Hitler, but firm and fair control will help progress. He or she should have the respect of the group and be a good oral communicator. Chapter 6 explains in more detail the skills of chairmanship required. He or she should understand fully the content on which the group has to make decisions. A chairman should be tolerant, though not over-indulgent, of others' shortcomings. There is some evidence which suggests that those with an introvert personality make better chairmen than extroverts, because they are more likely to be able to bring others into the discussion rather than seeking to dominate it themselves. This is in contrast with normal practice since it is usually those who have the most to say for themselves who are thrust into the position of leadership which being a chairman implies.

Thinking ahead even at this stage to the form of minutes to be used, it is better to decide to record mainly the decisions taken with only a brief summary of the highlights of the discussion. Some groups record decisions only and, indeed, this does simplify matters and avoids people coming along afterwards seeking to modify what they are stated to have said. The group needs to give careful thought to what is *necessary*. Anything more will cause more problems than it solves. However, in those rare circumstances where a verbatim account is required it should not be shied away from.

Once the purpose of the meeting has been specified and once the other preliminaries and preconditions have been thought about, you will be ready to proceed to the next stage which is concerned with the detailed preparation for the meeting. In the foregoing, as in what follows, concentrate on the items which affect you directly as they are likely to vary from meeting to meeting as your own role changes. Refer to the relevant items in the checklist in Chapter 17 on each occasion.

Types of meetings

Meetings can be classified in various ways – according to form and function, according to content or according to the degree of formality. There is no standard pattern. It will, however, be helpful to us if we classify some of the main ones according to purpose, as follows:

1   Executive (or command) meetings
These are the kinds of meetings most commonly found day-to-day in business, industrial or public service organisations. They exist to pass orders or instructions down the chain of command. Usually the person who calls the meeting makes the decisions and is consequently accountable for them. He decides who will attend and how the work is to be carried out. Such meetings are therefore essentially authoritarian and, if used at all, are most suitable for those matters where little or no discussion and debate are necessary or desirable.

2   Discussion (or consultative or advisory) meetings
Such meetings are called to exchange information and ideas, to explore problems or issues, or to talk around a subject in order to achieve a better understanding of it. They are not usually so much concerned with seeing that action results or that decisions are made. Everyone is encouraged to participate freely and to contribute whatever he has to offer. Meetings like this need to be very carefully structured and intelligently led if they are not to degenerate into meandering 'talking shops' which irritate and frustrate rather than help and serve.

3   Colleague meetings
When people of similar status or professional knowledge and expertise meet together they usually do so to bring each other up to date, to resolve a common problem or to settle a difference of

opinion on a course of action. Decisions are normally made by consensus rather than by vote or by one person, as in executive meetings. Consideration of topics will be on the basis of facts and rational arguments, although, as in all meetings, less praiseworthy methods of persuasion may be used. However, professionals are better at spotting when someone is trying to take them down a hazardous path precisely because of their specialist knowledge of the subject.

4 Committee meetings

In committees, people who represent various interests or groups meet together to make decisions on matters of common concern. These decisions will normally be made on the basis of a vote in which the majority side wins the day. If the votes for and against are tied, the chairman has an additional casting vote (see Chapter 16) to resolve the issue. Committees are our traditional democratic method of making decisions and are most common in local authorities, clubs and societies, and other activities in which all members are regarded as being equally entitled to take part in decisions.

5 Bargaining (or negotiation or trading) meetings

In such meetings, people come together to secure something of mutual advantage. Each side has to feel that it has something to gain for the meeting to succeed. Ideally, if each side feels it has achieved the better of the deal, everyone will leave the meeting happy, regardless of the true nature of the outcome. Decisions need to be generally agreed and supported or else the meeting will have been a waste of everybody's time. Very often those involved will need to meet several times before difficult points of dispute can be resolved. They may even call in a mediator if a deadlock has been reached to see if someone impartial can help them to find a mutually acceptable way around an impasse.

6 Progress (or review) meetings

These are common in business and industry and often take the form of reports on progress made by individuals responsible for specific parts of a larger project or even for specific activities within an organisation. Site meetings at construction works and routine Monday morning management team meetings are examples. They are usually chaired by the most senior person present and are designed particularly to aid early identification of possible problems or difficulties. This then makes speedy preventative or remedial action much easier to implement.

All of these meetings can be conducted formally (that is, according to strict rules and procedures) or informally (that is, with much more flexibility) depending upon the nature of the organisation, the purposes of the meeting or the personality of the chairman. It is useful to identify the types of meetings you have to attend as this helps to increase awareness of and familiarity with the context within which you have to operate. This contributes to the development of better performance and helps to improve confidence in dealing with different types of meetings.

3

Action Before a Meeting

As soon as you know you have to attend a meeting, whether the notice arrives in the post well in advance or by means of a telephone call a few minutes beforehand, you have to decide: are you going to attend or not? Of course, sometimes you will have no choice, perhaps because your boss has called the meeting, but often you will. Your decision will depend on many factors, such as competing claims upon your time, whether the subject of the meeting is one that attracts you, or whether you have something particular to gain by attending.

If you decide not to attend, you will usually need to apologise for your absence. For an informal meeting, it may be sufficient to do this orally, perhaps by telephone. For a formal meeting it will be more usual to apologise in writing. You could, of course, simply stay away and say nothing, but this is discourteous and does nothing to improve your image in the eyes of others.

Let us suppose you decide to attend and let us further suppose that the meeting you have been summoned to is a meeting of a committee of a local authority of which you are an officer or maybe a member. This example will enable us to relate the general principles of preparing for meetings to a specific real-life context and should therefore help you to understand them more readily and consequently apply them more effectively in your own meetings.

There are special tasks of chairmen, secretaries and treasurers to complete in advance for meetings. These will be covered in Chapters 6, 7 and 15 respectively. This chapter deals with matters which everyone who attends a meeting has to see to beforehand.

Objectives

As with most activities at work, it helps if you have specific objectives to achieve by attending a meeting. It is important here to bear in mind the difference between aims and objectives. Aims are rather vague and general, like hopes and aspirations. Objectives are specific and measurable or quantifiable, like targets and quotas. An aim, if you like, tells you the direction in which you intend to proceed. An objective tells you how far in that direction you intend to proceed, usually within a given time frame.

So the question you have to ask yourself is: what do you want from the meeting? You may want the meeting to reach a particular decision or to agree upon a certain course of action. You may want it to help you to solve a problem that you or some other participants have. On the other hand, you may simply wish to give your views on some of the topics being considered. Or you may merely want to go along to see what other people have to say.

Whatever it is that you want from a meeting, it will assist you in participating effectively if you can identify it in advance. This will be even more useful to you if you can write it down, preferably in a single sentence. If you have several objectives, however, it may be better to set them down as a numbered list. Then, during the meeting, you can tick off each objective as it has been achieved.

For example, in a local government committee meeting, your list of objectives might be:

1 Query the accuracy of the minutes of the last meeting on item 12.
2 Speak in support of item 3.
3 Speak against item 6.
4 Ask for more information about the proposed shopping centre development in your ward.
5 Ask if the treasurer has assessed the financial implications of item 10.
6 Ask how many people will be attending the conference in Bordeaux and what the total cost to the ratepayers will be.

From this, you can see that, whatever the precise content of the numbered items, you will be able to keep track of exactly what you should be doing at any point in the meeting. The list will also be useful during the kind of pre-meeting lobbying discussed later in this chapter.

Key agenda items

Not everything a meeting has to consider is of equal importance. Some items will be of key significance and it is desirable to identify those in advance if you can. Usually the key items or issues will comprise areas of controversy, difficult decisions, unpleasant decisions or finely balanced issues in which it is not clear which position is the best one to take.

Areas of controversy in local government committee meetings often relate to those matters on which there are political differences among the members. On most district and county councils, the people elected will be members of one of the major political parties. Each party has its own policies on a wide range of issues and, since these frequently conflict with the policies of other parties, controversy is inevitable. Even on councils where independent members dominate, there will be local issues – such as whether or not to give planning permission for a large grain silo or to build a new road – which will be controversial.

Difficult decisions will frequently involve matters where there are competing claims upon resources, for example. A committee may wish to spend £50 000 to assist a local industrialist to set up a factory and to spend £50 000 on an access road to attract a new business into the area. If it only has £50 000 left in its budget, it has the unenviable task of deciding which project to support. Limited resources always make for difficult decisions.

Unpleasant decisions may include the suspension or dismissal of an officer for misconduct or because of redundancy. Personnel problems are especially prone to result in unpleasant decisions.

Finely balanced issues are very common in local government, as elsewhere. Few matters are black or white and most involve various shades of grey. An industrialist may apply for a grant to help him stay in business and thus preserve the jobs of his employees, but there may well be serious doubts as to whether or not the injection of the amount requested will keep the company afloat. It may even be that less money than that being asked for will be sufficient.

Judging where the balance may be tipped one way or the other is not an easy task and a mistake can be expensive.

Whatever it is that makes an item a key item, identify it and you can then tell what must have priority when it comes to the next step of planning your approach to the meeting.

Planning an approach

In addition to setting yourself objectives and identifying the key agenda items, you need to clarify your expectations of how the meeting will proceed and plan accordingly. If you wish to speak on several items and you expect the meeting to be crowded, you will need to turn up early and select a seat from which you can easily 'catch the chairman's eye'. If you are merely keeping 'a watching brief' on events, a seat out of the way at the back may suffice.

You will need to make notes on what you are going to say. We shall cover this point more fully in Chapter 5, but early identification of key words and phrases which will remind you of what to say is most helpful. For major contributions you will find it useful to write out your speech in full and then make notes from that. The knowledge that you have your speech in your pocket if you dry up gives a great boost to your confidence.

Put the agenda items in your own priority order. It is very rare to find that the agenda as printed agrees with your own assessment of what is important. It is particularly necessary to look for things which are important to you but which are tucked away in a mass of other information. This can only be done effectively in the context of a planned approach. Relying upon luck or chance in spotting key items is not sufficient.

It is desirable to select a limited number of items to deal with. Chairmen (and, indeed, committees as a whole) can become very irritated with someone who pops up on every topic to put in his twopennyworth. Pick out the things that really matter to you. You may even ask other members to raise less important matters.

Plans help to focus activity, but they can go wrong. In fact, it is unlikely that any meeting will proceed exactly as you expect. Therefore, you need an alternative plan in case the first one proves inappropriate. To develop this, examine each of your priority items and ask yourself: what do I do if things do not go according to plan? Your answers to this question provide you with your 'Plan B'.

In meetings where you know other participants will want things which conflict with what you want, you may have to compromise. In such a case, it is desirable to identify a fallback position in advance as this helps in measuring the costs of any concessions you are compelled to make. This is a common feature of meetings in which any kind of bargaining, bidding or negotiating is taking place. It is also worth specifying a 'wall' position beyond which you are not prepared to be pushed. If you are pressed beyond this point, you may well have to resign from the committee as a matter of principle. The more clearly you can see the consequences of the various possible outcomes, the more easily you can determine your position at any point in the meeting and the more effectively you can operate within it.

Briefing yourself

Secretaries or, in local authorities, committee administrators often produce briefing notes for the chairman. Other members do not normally have this assistance and therefore have to develop techniques for briefing themselves. However, it is possible to give some advice on how to set about this which will reduce the time it takes and increase the usefulness of the end product.

Clearly, once you have completed the tasks we have already discussed in this chapter and once you have received the papers for the meeting, you will have to read those papers. This is the first essential step in the process of briefing yourself. How you will do this will depend upon your purpose in reading them.

If, for instance, you require a general understanding of what is contained in the papers (that is, you have not yet been able to identify particular things to look for) you should find it useful to follow these steps:

1   See how the material is organised. Let your eyes break away from the line-by-line approach of ordinary reading and move freely across and down the page (i.e. skim). Look for headings which indicate the pattern of organisation. They may be written in capital letters or they may even be labelled as 'Part A', 'Part B' and so on.

2 Once you can see how the writer has organised his material, skim the report, minutes or whatever it happens to be with a view to identifying the headings under which the main points are likely to be. If there are no headings, you will read the first sentence of each paragraph to help you decide. This is an effective technique because in a paragraph there are two positions of natural emphasis – the beginning and the end (because they are easier to see, either because the first line is indented or there are spaces between paragraphs). If a writer has something important to say, such as a main point, it is logical to put it in one of these positions of natural emphasis. In most paragraphs, the main point will be at the beginning, since this carries the greater emphasis.

3 Read (at an appropriate speed) any Summary, Conclusions and Recommendations sections which have been provided.

4 Read through the whole report, minutes, etc., paying most attention to the places identified during step 2 above.

5 Identify and mark problems with the text, but do not stop reading or go back to an earlier point until you have read through the text as a whole. The reason for this is that it is often easier to resolve difficulties in understanding something if you have an idea of the overall context and consequently of where the difficulty fits within that. If, as you read, you mark the material in the following ways, you will find that this helps not only in understanding and remembering what you have read, but also in locating particular points at some time in the future. In other words, it can save time during subsequent readings and even eliminate them altogether by enabling you to go straight to what you are looking for:

    I   This indicates a point of interest.
    II   This indicates a point of importance.
    III This indicates a point of vital importance.
    X   This indicates a statement you disagree with.
    √   This indicates a statement you agree with.
    ?   This indicates a statement you do not understand or that there is some other reason for doubt.

6 After you have finished reading a report, minutes, etc., put it to one side, take a blank sheet of paper and try to write down key points in your own words. The Americans call this technique

'self-recitation' and it has been shown to give far better recall of information a person wishes to remember than even three or four readings can provide.

7   Check your self-recitation with the original version to ensure accuracy.

8   Move on to the next piece of reading material.

If, on the other hand, you wish to find out whether or not some specific information is present in the material or not, that is, you are searching for something in particular, follow these steps:

1   See how the material is organised, as in the technique outlined above.

2   Organise the information you are looking for, that is to say, group items together to match the sections or divisions into which the writer has grouped what he has to say. Try to identify key words and phrases to look for which are likely to be in the material. If you have such key words and phrases in mind and if they are present, your eyes will tend to be drawn to them, in much the same way that your eyes seem to be drawn to what you are looking for when you peruse classified advertisements pages in newspapers.

3   Look first of all in the most promising sections or paragraphs as identified in step 1 above. Mark the location of the information or make a note of its whereabouts.

4   Mop up any remaining requirements by checking through any appendices or other possible sections or paragraphs which are present.

5   Read in full only if necessary.

6   Move on to the next piece of material.

If all you wish to do is to obtain the flavour of a piece of reading material and some idea of the kind of main points the writer is making, read the first sentence of each paragraph. It may also be worth reading the last sentence of long paragraphs. The effectiveness of this technique rests on the positions of natural emphasis referred to earlier.

Since committee members will often have great quantities of reading to do, it can be worthwhile setting aside some time to build up reading speeds. This can sometimes be achieved by keeping a record of reading speeds while trying to increase speeds gradually.

Reading speeds are conventionally measured in 'words per minute', as in typing. An approximation of the number of words will do (count the words in ten lines, divide by ten, multiply by the number of lines in the material). Comprehension can be tested by means of the kind of self-recitation described above. Those who would prefer a training course in the skills of rapid and efficient reading will find that the British Institute of Management conducts courses regularly in London. Those who find it more convenient to work at home will find *Rapid Reading Made Simple* by Gordon R. Wainwright (Heinemann) a useful text.

Really important materials which must be understood in depth require a study strategy. In this case, the following steps should be taken:

1 Skim to see how the material is organised.
2 Write down any key words or phrases which are relevant to the subject or questions for which you require answers.
3 Read the material at an appropriate speed. Remember that very slow speeds often mean that you will forget what you have read at the top of a page by the time you get to the bottom or that you will find it difficult to relate what you are reading now to what you have just read and to be able to anticipate what is likely to be coming next. It may be necessary to be prepared to read something more than once in order to understand it. In fact, difficult material is often easier to understand if you have first of all read it through in full quite quickly (even if that does not provide full comprehension). The overview thus provided makes it easier to sort out problems in understanding particular parts of the material.
4 Use self-recitation to test understanding. If what you are trying to test are inferences drawn, deductions made or conclusions arrived at, it may be better to wait for a while before testing. This kind of 'incubation period', as it is called, seems to help.
5 Revise the points or information to be remembered the same day and then at regular intervals until the meeting.

Research

In addition to briefing yourself on the papers for the meeting, it may sometimes be necessary to consult other sources of information.

You may need to use libraries and other sources of information. Members of local authorities may need to seek additional information from officers. Those who attend other kinds of meetings may need to assemble background information to broaden their grasp of the subject or to enable them to get all the facts together. Research can take many forms. Whatever form it does take, it is as well to allow some time for it in advance of a meeting.

It may also be useful to look at previous papers which have been before the committee. If an item has come up before, its fate could well be determined by what happened to it the last time. Committees are very much creatures of habit and tend to follow the precedents which their previous decisions have set. It may also be possible to identify items similar to the ones you are concerned with, and again their fates may give a clue to what will happen this time.

In collecting this kind of background information, how much can be done will depend not only on what is available, but also on how much time is at your disposal. Where time is particularly limited, you may have to decide on the real priorities for your attention. After all, no one can expect to become an expert in all the subjects a committee deals with. A degree of specialisation will often be necessary and desirable. Better to be a master of some trades than a jack of them all.

Lobbying

Sometimes, if there is an important matter on which you want a favourable decision (or even an unfavourable one) from a committee, it may be helpful to canvass some other members of the committee to find out what their thoughts are. This lobbying is quite common in local authorities. Likely sympathisers may be found among fellow party members or by looking at individuals' previous voting records.

Often, some members of a committee will be more influential than others and, if these key members can be identified and successfully approached to support you, your chances of getting the decision you want are greatly increased. It may also help if officers support the line you wish to take. Although it is the elected members who will be responsible for decisions, they frequently listen carefully to the advice they are given by the professionals.

The chairman may also be worth sounding out for, although chairmen are supposed to be impartial, this does not always apply to quite the full extent in local authorities and if the chairman is your ally that is a powerful force in your favour. When you are lobbying, it is advisable to explore every possibility there is for recruiting support. You may thus even be able to go into a meeting knowing in advance that, barring accidents, your view will prevail.

If you carry out all the steps recommended in this chapter before you attend a meeting, you will have taken a sizeable step towards ensuring your effective participation in it.

4

How a Meeting Proceeds

Many people, when they first begin to take an interest in how meetings operate and in how they may be run more effectively, assume that there is a body of rules which, once mastered, give them the secret of successful meetings. You should entertain no such misconceptions. No such golden and infallible rules exist. There are conventions which most people follow, and procedures which are common to a wide variety of meetings. But there are very few rules, if any, which cannot be broken if the circumstances and expediency require it.

Despite this absence of an unchallengeable body of law, as it were, about what must or must not be done, most meetings exhibit certain common characteristics. These characteristics lie in their conduct rather than their content. It may, therefore, be helpful if we consider at this point how a typical meeting proceeds.

Opening a meeting

So, once you get into a meeting, what happens? The first thing that has to happen, clearly, is for the meeting to begin. At the time appointed, the chairman will look around to see that a quorum (the minimum number of people needed for the meeting to take place – see below and Chapter 16) is present. Sometimes, meetings begin late, but even so the chairman still has to check that he has enough people to proceed. The only time he does not have to do this is when an organisation has not specified a quorum in its standing orders (again, see below and Chapter 16). Indeed, a judge has ruled that in some circumstances a meeting of one person can be a valid meeting.*

The chairman will then call the meeting to order and declare it open. He will read the agenda, unless copies of it have already been circulated round those present or have been sent to them in advance by post. He will then ask if any apologies for absence have been notified to the secretary or if anyone has asked someone present to give his apologies for him. Once he has completed these few formalities, the chairman will proceed to the first item on the agenda.

Working through the agenda

Every meeting has an agenda, or list of items for discussion and decision. Even where this is not written down, it will still exist – if only in the minds of the chairman or those present. The meeting will work its way through the items in the order in which they are listed. If, for instance, the chairman wants to take an item out of sequence, he should only do this with the approval of the rest of those present.

Normally, it will not be necessary to spend the same amount of time on each item. Some will need lengthy and thoroughgoing discussion whereas others will need little or none. The more items can be quickly agreed, the more time there will be for those where there are known to be serious differences of opinion amongst those present.

Once a matter has been dealt with by a meeting, it may not be raised again at that meeting. Often, organisations place a minimum time limit before the matter is placed on the agenda again. This is a sensible provision to prevent subsequent meetings being tied up in the discussion of one item while the rest of the organisation's business is neglected.

A meeting should not have too many items on the agenda and the secretary and the chairman, when they draw it up, should bear in mind their organisation's capacity for processing business. It is

* This ruling and many other examples of court rulings affecting committee procedure are given in *The Law and Procedure of Meetings* by R. R. Pitfield and P. F. Hughes (see Further Reading, p. 175).

better to increase the frequency of meetings rather than to have meetings which seem never-ending.

However, it should be possible for other members of the club or society, say, to place items on the agenda. An astute chairman will still be able to have an item taken off by asking the meeting if it wants to discuss it before he gives the initiator a chance to speak at length about it.

Order of items

Chapter 7 contains a detailed treatment of the construction of an agenda, but it will be useful for us to look at some of the basic principles here. There are some items which will normally appear, for example:

Minutes of the last meeting
Matters arising
Correspondence
Secretary's Report
Treasurer's Report
Any Other Business

Other items which are not regular, but which are related to the activities of the organisation at a particular point in time, may vary widely in nature. For instance, in a club or society, they may from time to time include plans for a:

Bring and Buy Sale
Christmas Social Evening
Visit of National President
Future Activities
Summer Fayre
Visiting Speaker
Film Show

and so on.

Regular items will have a fixed place on the agenda and will usually be taken first, with the exception of 'Any Other Business' which always comes last. The Chairman will proceed through them systematically in the same order at each meeting.

As far as non-regular items are concerned, the convention is that the more important ones are taken first. The reason for this is that, by the time the regular items have been dealt with, latecomers will have arrived and the meeting will have the maximum attendance for the main business. If some people have to leave early because of domestic or other commitments, they will still have a better chance of being present when the big decisions are being taken. It is not so vital that everyone should be present for minor matters. Also, leaving important items till last may make some members suspicious that the regular attenders are actually hoping that some people will have to leave before discussion takes place on them. It has been known, particularly in political organisations, for this device to be used to give greater decision-making power to the 'activists' who do not mind how long a meeting lasts. You should always resist attempts to take key decisions when people have begun to drift away from a meeting.

'Any Other Business' should contain minor items only. Under no circumstances should a chairman allow major matters to be brought up without prior warning. To do so is to invite criticism and disaffection amongst the membership. 'Any Other Business' is really a tidying-up item for those small things which will not fit easily under any other heading. If something is raised which clearly involves a major issue, it should be deferred for consideration at the next meeting, when it can be put on the agenda in its own right. One useful protection against a possible abuse of AOB is to have a rule that no motion may be moved on an item raised.

The quorum

The *quorum* is the number of people who must be present before a meeting can legally make decisions. Normally, this is at least two people, but many organisations specify a larger number such as a quarter or a third of the members.

A quorum is important not only because decisions may later be invalidated if a club or society is taken to court over a disputed decision, but also because it prevents a small clique running matters without making an effort to involve other members. It is particularly important in formal meetings such as a club's Annual General Meeting.

Most of the standard texts on meetings recommend that organisations should specify the quorum for meetings in their rules. It is also as well to remember that the quorum must be maintained for the whole meeting. If the attendance drops below the minimum for part of the meeting, decisions made during that period will be invalid. Some people believe wrongly, that this only applies if the quorum is challenged – that is, if someone says the minimum number of people are no longer present. However, if the rules of the organisation specifically define a quorum in terms of the number 'present at the time when the meeting proceeds to business' (i.e. begins), it has been held in court that the quorum, if achieved at the beginning of the meeting, can be assumed to last for the whole meeting.* Usually, the beginning of the meeting means that a club can wait up to half an hour for sufficient members to turn up before a meeting is abandoned. Such a meeting is usually adjourned for one week so that another attempt can be made to achieve a quorum.

The quorum is thus an important safeguard which should be taken much more seriously than it often is. Every time a club or society turns a blind eye when a quorum is not present, it is undermining one of the basic principles of democratic involvement in an organisation's affairs.

Framing motions

Before a proposal has been decided upon, it is a *motion*. Once a decision has been made, it becomes a *resolution*. This may seem an unnecessary and pedantic distinction but at least it has the merit of indicating the relative status of various proposals. It is also possible to have a *notice of motion* – in other words, a proposal which is to be put to the following meeting of an organisation so that members have time or notice to consider it properly. Sometimes such notices can be taken at a meeting as *emergency motions*, but this should only be done when there is genuine urgency.

The convention is that motions are framed positively rather than negatively. This is sensible because, if a motion is subsequently amended, it is easier for members to follow the changes. Negatively worded statements are, in any case, more difficult to understand

---

* This ruling is cited in *The Law and Procedure of Meetings*, by Pitfield and Hughes (see Further Reading, p. 175).

than positive ones. Research has shown that much more brain activity is required to understand negative statements, but why this should be so is not clear. It is thought that the brain may need to convert a negative statement into a positive one in order to understand it, and that this may account for the increased activity.

It is thus better to frame a motion in the following terms:

> 'That the Annual Dinner be held on Friday 17 December at the Seaburn Hotel.'

rather than to phrase it:

> 'That the Annual Dinner should not be held on Friday 17 December at the Seaburn Hotel.'

The second version leaves it vague as to whether the objection is to the date and venue or to the very idea of having an Annual Dinner at all. It is also more difficult to amend to produce a clear statement of what action is to be taken.

Motions should be in writing. This enables everybody to be clear about what is being proposed. If necessary, a chairman should be asked to allow time for a motion to be written out and then read aloud to the meeting. Far better, though, if motions can be written down and circulated before a meeting takes place.

Amendments

When a motion is being discussed, it may be changed or *amended*. A proposal to amend will usually need a seconder, and during debate on it comments must be restricted to the amendment. The motion is put to one side until the amendment has been voted on and won or lost. If the amendment is carried, the motion is changed accordingly and the new form of words becomes the substantive motion.

The wording of an amendment can change the meaning of a motion, but it cannot contradict it. Anyone who is directly opposed to the motion can speak and vote against it, but those who are only partly opposed (or partly in agreement) have to have the facility for proposing amendments. Amendments propose changes by doing one of four things:

(*a*) omitting words;
(*b*) substituting words;

(*c*)   inserting words;

(*d*)   combining any of these.

Whilst there may be only one motion under discussion at any one time, there may be several amendments and the chairman will decide in which order to take them. It is even possible to amend an amendment. The second amendment is simply discussed first and, if carried, incorporated into the first amendment.

Let us take an example of amending a motion. Suppose the motion is the one in the previous section, a possible amendment might be:

> 'That everything after "on" should be deleted and replaced by the words "Saturday 18 December at the Roker Hotel".'

An amendment to the amendment might be:

> 'That "the Roker Hotel" be replaced by "the Seaburn Hotel".'

It is important to remember that an amendment must specify precisely which words from the motion or other amendment are to be omitted or substituted by others, or which words are to be inserted and where.

Reaching decisions

A meeting has at least five ways of reaching and recording its decisions:

(*a*)   by a show of hands;

(*b*)   by ballot;

(*c*)   by a generally expressed consensus of views;

(*d*)   by allowing the chairman to judge the sense of the meeting; and

(*e*)   by allowing the chairman to take its silence as agreement with the proposal under discussion.

Each of these methods has its advantages and disadvantages.

A show of hands is quick and offers a clear picture of how a meeting feels. Some people do not like this method because it means everyone can see how everyone else voted. It makes later recriminations easier if some of the members think a person should have voted with them and he has not.

A ballot takes longer, but has the advantage of being secret. The problem with ballots is that, if there are too many of them – as in the election of officers at the AGM, for instance – they can slow a meeting down to a virtual standstill.

A consensus view can be taken when no one has spoken against a proposal, and even if they have, provided they withdraw their objections at some point. If no one has then spoken against a proposal after they have had every opportunity to do so, a chairman can reasonably infer that a majority of the meeting is in support. The converse, when everyone speaks against, also applies.

Some meetings are prepared to go further than this and allow the chairman to take 'the sense of the meeting' and pronounce accordingly. In doing this, the chairman considers how many people appear to be in favour and how strongly, and how many are against and how strongly. He then rules on whether the proposal is carried or not. It should still be open, however, for anyone who is strongly opposed to his ruling to have the matter put to the vote by show of hands or ballot.

In a few circumstances, it may be possible for a chairman to assume that silence on the part of those present indicates agreement with a proposal. This is more common in informal business meetings or club and society meetings than anywhere else.

Whatever method is used, a meeting must have a method of showing it has made a decision. Unless this is done, confusion is almost certain to arise at some time in the future.

It is often possible to tell when a meeting has reached the point at which it is ready to make a decision on a proposal or motion. People tend to go quiet and may even begin to get restless or show signs of impatience with anyone who continues speaking about the proposal. This situation does not arise immediately but only when a meeting feels that it has heard a representative selection of views for and against. A good chairman will not need to wait until someone proposes that the motion be put, but will be sensitive to cues like these and bring the discussion to an end.

Rules of debate

If you expect to find that there is somewhere a set of fixed rules which control how debate in a meeting is to be conducted, you will be disappointed. The rules used in the British houses of Parliament form the basis of the rules followed in most meetings, but they are not rules which have any legal force. They provide for such things as how motions can be placed before a meeting, how they should be proposed and seconded, how a person received permission from the chair to speak, how and when a person speaking may be interrupted, and so on.

Many of these rules will be stated in a club's or society's *standing orders*. These should cover, amongst other things:

(*a*) the quorum needed for business to be legally done;
(*b*) the order of items of business;
(*c*) how standing orders may be suspended, if necessary;
(*d*) how minutes of previous meetings may be discussed (if at all);
(*e*) how a chairman's ruling may be challenged;
(*f*) how long the speeches may be and whether a person may speak more than once;
(*g*) how motions and amendments are proposed and seconded;
(*h*) how discussion may be ended or adjourned;
(*i*) how votes are taken;
(*j*) the notice needed for putting a motion on an agenda;
(*k*) when a motion may be withdrawn (usually, once a motion has been proposed and seconded, it becomes the property of the meeting and no longer belongs to its proposers);
(*l*) how much notice is needed to call a meeting, together with the rules for calling the annual general meetings and extraordinary general meetings.

Standing orders may be ignored in informal meetings, but they should not be set aside lightly. They provide a structure within which civilised discussion and decision-making may take place. They keep meetings orderly and productive. A specimen of standing orders can be seen in Chapter 16.

Points of order

Points of order are challenges to the way a meeting is being conducted; that is, the persons raising them are in effect saying that the chairman is not following the organisation's rules of procedure. When these are raised, they must be concerned with how a meeting is being conducted and they must be dealt with straight away. They take precedence over all other business and a chairman may not legally ignore a point of order.

Thus, it would seem that they should be easy for people who attend meetings to understand. Yet this is not the case. Many people who raise a point of order will try to use the opportunity of gaining the floor to make a speech. Both chairman and other participants should resist this vigorously, as the result will be total confusion if someone is allowed to use a procedural motion to comment on the content of a proposal.

Points of order are often confused with points of information, to which a speaker does not have to give way. Asking a question or supplying information does not constitute a point of order. Many organisations wisely make no provision for points of information in their rules. This helps to preserve the point of order as a means of challenging only the conduct of the business, and not its content.

Procedural motions

The procedural motions that are most likely to be encountered as a club or society meeting proceeds are:

(a) '*That the motion be now put.*' This is proposed when it is thought that the discussion has gone on long enough and a vote should now be taken.

(b) '*That the motion be not put.*' Sometimes referred to as 'the previous question', this motion is designed to avoid taking a firm decision one way or another. The matter may then be brought up again at a subsequent meeting without waiting for the customary six months before matters on which a decision has been taken can be raised. It can also help a meeting to avoid making a difficult or embarrassing decision.

(c) '*That the chairman's ruling be upheld.*' This is the motion debated when someone challenges a chairman's ruling. Usually the secretary takes the chair until the motion has been voted on. If it is defeated, a chairman will often resign forthwith, so the secretary may remain in the chair until a new chairman is elected. The motion normally needs a two-thirds majority to succeed.

Closing a meeting

Once all the business has been dealt with, including 'Any Other Business', the chairman will close the meeting. He may ask again if there is any other business, just to give members one last chance to raise any minor matters not covered by any other item on the agenda. If there are none, the chairman reminds everyone of the date, time and place of the next meeting (assuming these have been fixed) and then declares the present meeting closed. He may, finally, tell the secretary at what time the meeting has closed so that he or she can record it in the minutes. The meeting is then at an end and the members can disperse or, more frequently, repair to the bar for refreshments.

5

How to Participate in a Meeting

Sometimes your association with an organisation begins at the beginning. You are present at its creation and attend the inaugural meeting. You are a founder member, with all that implies in terms of status and ability to influence decisions or, at the very least, have people listen to your point of view. You are a participant from the start.

Most of the time, however, the organisations you become associated with – be they clubs, societies, companies or local councils – will already have been in existence for some time. They will have their own rules, procedures and conventions and you will have to understand and master them before you can become an effective participant. Your first role will, therefore, be as observer and learner. One of the purposes of this book, and particularly of this chapter, is to make that period of 'waiting in the wings' before you are ready to enter into the fray as brief as possible.

As soon as you join an organisation, and even before you are called to attend any meetings, find out as much as you can about what it has done in the past. Find out what kinds of decisions it has made. This information will be available in the minutes of previous meetings. In the case of local councils, the public library should be able to help. With most organisations, it helps to talk to long-standing members. Their personal recollections will often go beyond mere facts to all sorts of other fascinating insights into how decisions have been made. If you can talk to several such people, you will quickly become aware of established attitudes to certain subjects, of prejudices, of preferred patterns of working, of achievements and failures, and much more. It is always worth remembering that people are a rich source of information.

When you are called to a meeting, find out who will be present. This is important because, very often, decisions are influenced, and in some cases determined, by who turns up. You should try to identify the key opinion leaders who will be present at the meeting, and try to find out as much as possible about these people. If you have done your preparation properly, along the lines proposed in Chapter 3, and you discover that some opinion leaders have broadly the same views on a subject to be discussed as yourself, it can help to mention this to them in advance. At best they will discuss the matter with you in some detail and may even suggest how you might usefully contribute to the discussions, and at the very least they should be pleased to learn that they have another ally. Those who are the leaders when it comes to forming opinions, and thus influencing decisions in organisations, are usually very keen to identify potential supporters for their views. That is part of what politics, whether it has a capital 'P' or not, is all about and opinion leaders in any organisation are invariably 'politicians'.

Being ready

We have already discussed general preparation for attending meetings in Chapter 3. Here we shall consider preparation from the specific standpoint of being able to make a useful contribution to the proceedings.

If you know that you are going to make a contribution to a meeting, or even if you only have an idea that you might contribute if all goes well, it makes sense to be ready in advance. This means that there are certain steps you need to progress through so that you are in a position to speak out with the minimum of risk of making a fool of yourself.

The first step is to define for yourself some terms of reference. In other words, ask yourself questions like these:

(*a*)   What are the general aims of the meeting?
(*b*)   What is the main subject of the meeting?
(*c*)   Who will attend the meeting?
(*d*)   What do I wish to achieve by attending?

The second step is to make some assessment of the audience at the meeting. To do this, you should ask yourself questions like:

(*a*)   What is the subject on which I intend to speak? (If there is more than one, you may need to carry out this audience analysis more than once.)

(*b*)   What do those attending the meeting know about the subject already?

(*c*)   Do they have any known opinions about the subject?

(*d*)   What do I need to tell them about the subject?

(*e*)   What assumptions are they likely to have made? What assumptions have I made?

(*f*)   What response or reaction do I want from them?

Thirdly, you need to define for yourself, as precisely as you can, a set of objectives to be achieved. These can be assembled from the answers to the above and other questions, so that a reasonably typical set of objectives for a meeting might read like those on page 25.

You can then collect the information you need in order to satisfy these objectives.

Making notes

In collecting information, it helps if you have a system for making notes which enables you to record the *maximum amount in the minimum space*. Most people develop their own methods during the years they spend at school and college, but for those who have not had either the opportunity or the need to devise a system of their own, a reasonably simple one can be suggested.

The first thing to do when trying to reduce the amount that needs writing down is to omit the vowels from words. This can be done because most of the distinguishing characteristics of words are to be found in the consonants. For example, if instead of:

Now is the time for all good men to rally to the aid of the party

you write:

nw s th tm fr ll gd mn t rlly t th d f th prty

you have reduced fifty letters to thirty-one – a reduction of 38 per cent. Some of the abbreviations are unsatisfactory, however, such as 'll' for 'all' and 'd' for 'aid'. For this reason, we need some other steps to provide us with a little flexibility.

The next step is to omit unnecessary words. In the example given above, we can probably reduce that to:

Now time all good men rally aid party.

Sixteen words are thus reduced to eight.

We can go further. We can shorten long words, if there are any. That will not apply here, but would if words like 'information' (info), 'specification' (spec) or 'necessary' (nec) were present. We can have special abbreviations for common words. For example, 's' for 'is', 'l' for 'all', and '→' for 'to'. We can have abbreviations for other frequently used words, such as 'cont' for 'continued', 'arr' for 'arrival' and 'pty' for 'party'. To complete the set of simple techniques for reducing the amount that needs to be written down, we can use the note form of expression. In other words, identify the key points, eliminate everything that is secondary to this, omit qualifying phrases as far as possible and change the construction of the material if this will enable the point to be made more simply.

Using all of these points, or as many as are relevant to this example, we may reduce our original statement to:

Nw tm gd ♂ rly pty.

(♂ can be used as a symbol for all male references; ♀ for female). Fifty letters are thus reduced to thirteen letters and a symbol – a reduction of 74 per cent. This illustrates the fact that the approach is flexible. A technique does not have to be applied if there is a better way. For instance, 'ai' is a better contraction for 'aid' than 'd'. The fact that someone else may not understand your contractions does not matter, because you are making notes for your own use and it is sufficient that you should understand. Indeed, the same contractions can be used on different occasions (for example, 'cont') because the context will enable you to tell exactly what it is short for (for example, 'continuity', 'contingency', or 'contamination'). If you wish to take a closer look at this method of notemaking, you will find it described in detail in *People and Communication Workbook* by Gordon R. Wainwright (Macdonald & Evans, pages 1–9).

Early participation

If you are intending to play an active part in a meeting, it helps if you participate early. Why this should be so is not clear, but it seems to be the case. It may be that, if you take part early, you are more likely to feel that you are an integral part of the meeting and therefore fully entitled to have your say. *Early participation helps to build confidence.*

If you are the kind of person who needs his or her confidence building up, the chances are that you will frequently need it building up. Do not assume that once confidence has been acquired it will remain with you forever. This is not the case. It is quite natural for confidence to need regular reinforcement. Never become complacent. If you feel in need of a little boost to your ego, remind yourself to find some pretext on which you can make an early contribution to a meeting – even if it is on a quite trivial matter, like a small correction to the minutes or a minor matter arising from the minutes. You will soon find how well this simple little technique works.

Presenting a case

It is not within the scope of this book to offer comprehensive advice on what to do when you are speaking in public. There are plenty of books available which will do that and some of the more useful ones are listed in the Further Reading section. Nevertheless, some advice will be helpful in enabling you to put an argument to a meeting with a better chance of its succeeding.

When you speak, speak from notes. If you are making a lengthy presentation (five minutes or more), write out your introduction in full and memorise it. Remember that if you want to overcome possible objections to your point of view you will need to show your listeners that you understand their point of view. You will need to offer possibilities they can relate to and you will need to make your own proposals as clear as possible. Use simple words and do not mumble. If you are an officer presenting a case to a committee of elected members, or someone in business presenting a proposal to professional colleagues, or are in some other similar situation, *remember the value of visual aids.* If information can be better conveyed in visual form, then that is the way to do it. And give your listeners the necessary minimum when it comes to statistics. People listening to someone speaking find it very difficult to assimilate very much in the way of statistical information.

Identify the common ground that exists, if there is any, between your listeners and yourself, and build upon it. There is little point in fruitless arguments over set positions. It is better to use what is agreed between opposing sides to develop open mindedness and a willingness to consider new ideas and approaches.

Above all, *practise*. This is another simple technique for building confidence. The better you remember what it is that you want to say, the less danger there is of 'drying up' and not knowing what to say next. Practise before a mirror. Better still, read what you are going to say into a tape recorder and then listen to yourself. Best of all, if the facility is available to you, make a video-recording of yourself and then play it back. This method enables you to see not only what you say, but also how you say it.

Using body language

Most people assume that, because meetings rely heavily upon the spoken word as a means of communicating, nonverbal aspects (or body language) are less important. This is not so. Research has established that up to 93 per cent of the impact of a face-to-face encounter is nonverbal and only 7 per cent is verbal. It has also been established that where spoken langauge and body language conflict (that is, your words are saying one thing, but your body language is saying another), it is the body language which will be believed. So you cannot afford to neglect your body language in meetings.

It is particularly useful when it comes to getting a word in edgeways. If you know that you will wish to speak, you will find it much easier to do this if you sit where the chairman can easily see you. Positioning is an aspect of nonverbal communication which is not to be neglected.

'Catching the chairman's eye' is a phrase used to indicate the wish of a person to speak. It means that you first have to *establish eye contact* with the chairman and know that he is attending to you before you can give any other signals to communicate your intention. You can, of course, raise a hand or stand up or speak out, but there are many occasions on which these methods will be inappropriate, especially in smaller and less formal meetings. Looking steadily at the chairman and waiting to be noticed can be quite effective, as most people looking around a room will be aware if someone is clearly waiting in this way. Eyes tend to be attracted to eyes.

The effect can be reinforced by the *appropriate facial expression.* Slightly raised eyebrows, as in questioning, will indicate a desire to communicate. Even a slight smile may help as, in stressful situations like meetings, even the toughest chairman may welcome a friendly face to turn to. It has to be the slight smile of welcome, however. An inane grin will not do the trick.

Head position can help. If the head is slightly raised, this will underline the message of the slightly raised eyebrows. It will in any event make your face easier to see, especially if there are a large number of people present.

Holding up the hand slightly, perhaps with a pen or pencil in it, may sometimes be useful. The instrument makes the hand appear to be raised further than it is, so that you may be noticed without having to appear too pushy, as you might if you held your hand up higher. Some chairman react negatively to people who make it too obvious that they want to speak and studiously ignore them.

The right kind of posture can help. Sitting upright with some forward lean will not only help to raise your profile above those who are sitting back or leaning in a relaxed way to one side, but it will also serve to show your wish to enter the discussion. If it does not work the first time, sit back, wait for another suitable opportunity and, when the chairman is looking your way, move the top half of your body forward again.

Proximity and orientation can have an effect. Not only should you be sitting where the chairman can see you, you should also sit near to him and face him as directly as possible. It is possible to ignore people when they are right under our noses, but it does make it just that little bit more difficult.

In very small, informal meetings, it may even on occasion be appropriate to *reach out and touch* the chairman on the forearm to signal that you want his attention. It would, however, have to be a very informal meeting for this to work and your personal relationship with the chairman would have to be a very close and friendly one.

Appearance can influence who is attended to. Chairmen will tend to ignore people whose dress does not conform to the accepted organisational norm. Turn up in sweater and jeans when everyone else is wearing smart suits and ties and you should not be surprised if you are given less opportunity to speak than usual. You may even be ignored altogether.

Timing can be critical. If you study meetings and observe who are the people who are able to get a word in most often and most easily, you will find they time their interventions to perfection. They will signal their wish to speak and begin speaking almost simultaneously and their words will begin exactly as the previous speaker's have ended. Wait for a gap in the discussion and you may wait forever, so perfect will be the 'dovetailing' of contributions. However, if you observe for a while you will begin to sense the best moments for intervening. You will become aware that the discussion has a rhythm. Once you have identified this, you will have taken a major step towards developing better timing yourself and to being able to synchronise your own contributions with those of other people.

Once you have secured 'the floor', body language is important in helping you to put your point across. As you are speaking, you should establish eye contact with as many of your audience as possible. That is to say, your gaze should sweep around your listeners so that you look at as many of them as possible. In doing this, it is important not to neglect the extremes, that is, the people at the extreme left and extreme right of your sweep. By doing this you are more likely to give your audience the feeling that you are talking *to* them rather than *at* them. No audience likes to be talked at as if it did not really matter whether they were there or not.

Your face should exhibit *positive expressions*. Smiles and a lively, changing face are better than a motionless solemnity. You do not need to strive too hard to achieve this for, if you do the other things that are suggested here, your face will quite naturally adopt the kinds of expressions that will help to communicate to your audience the interest you feel in your subject and the desire you have to talk to them about it.

Keep your head up when you are talking to a group of people. If you do not, your voice will tend to fall as well, your tone will drop and you will begin to lose the attention of your listeners. The mere fact of keeping your head up helps your voice to carry without your having to raise the volume of your speech. Everyone likes to hear what a speaker has to say, but no audience likes to be shouted at.

Gestures should be open and expressive. This is, with the palms held outwards and thus visible to your listeners. Don't strive for artificially dramatic gestures, simply let your hand and other bodily movements form a natural punctuation to your words. At all costs, avoid gestures like scratching your head, or feeling your chin (especially if you have a beard) or moving your hands repeatedly in and out of your pockets.

When you are talking to a group of more than about twenty people, it can often be better to stand up to say whatever you have to say. The reason is that your voice will carry further and more easily. You need to remember that in many rooms the acoustics are not necessarily designed to let the human voice carry. If you do stand up, make sure that your posture is reasonably erect. You do not want to look as if you have a stair rod stuck down the back of your jacket, but neither do you want to look as if you are slouching and trying to look as if you are actually sitting down.

Face your audience directly when you are speaking to them. Remember the advice given to actors on stage always to look at the audience, or the more humorous, but nonetheless useful, advice given to teachers not to turn their backs on the kids because that's when they get up to mischief. Turn your back on your audience and that is when their attention will wander, they will begin to doodle and may even begin to talk amongst themselves. If this last happens, don't fall into the trap of raising your voice in order to regain attention. Far better to stop talking. The silence, sudden and unexpected, will re-direct attention to you. You can then begin talking again with the full attention of your audience guaranteed – at least for a while.

This brings us to the value of timing when speaking to a group. Time the pause right and it heightens the effect of what you have just said. *Never be afraid to pause.* Many inexperienced speakers assume that it is an indication of 'drying up' and they tend to panic. Audiences need pauses. If you continue relentlessly and without respite, your listeners will make their own pauses in what you say by letting their minds wander.

The elements of body language which have been looked at here can be used for many other purposes than getting a word in edgeways or getting your points across. They can help in contributing to discussions generally, in spotting receptivity and even opposition to what you have to say, in detecting deception when others are speaking, in seeing through to the 'hidden agenda' in a meeting, in identifying allies in your cause, in spotting leaders (those people to whom everyone seems to defer), and in telling when someone is not listening (even when someone is doodling they may still be listening).

You may find it helpful to *observe others' body language* in meetings occasionally, as well as to review your own use of it. Observe it part by part of the body, much as we considered it in this section. You might even find it useful to bear in mind the most useful kinds of body language for most purposes:

Eye contact It is better generally to use more rather than less. Look at people as often and as much as you reasonably can without overdoing it. Do not avoid eye contact when people you are meeting with clearly prefer to have more eye contact. Do not stare, of course, but remember that more eye contact is likely to lead to greater liking, greater awareness and more understanding of people.

Facial expressions These should be lively and expressive rather than too carefully controlled and restricted. Even unattractive people can appear attractive if they have lively faces.

Head movements Head nods, especially, are useful when listening. They show people you are attending to what they say. Increase them and people will actually talk more. Stop them and you may well cause someone to stop talking altogether. Try it sometime.

Gestures These should be open and expressive, without being artificially so. Avoid defensive, barrier gestures, like folding your arms across your chest, especially when speaking. Palm up or palm outward gestures are particularly useful to encourage confidence in yourself. On the other hand, note that high status speakers often make very few gestures and may even speak with their hands clasped loosely behind their backs.

Posture This should be reasonably erect with a little forward lean (as this tends to show interest in others and in what is going on generally). Leaning back or to one side can sometimes be useful if you wish to make someone else feel more relaxed and at ease in an informal meeting. Avoid stoop and slouch as these almost always produce negative reactions towards you in the minds of others.

Proximity and orientation   Where there is scope, get as near to people as you reasonably can. We tend, in the Western world, to keep our distance, yet there is plenty of evidence to indicate that if people are physically close together they are much more likely to think of themselves as being psychologically and intellectually close together. Direct orientations – for example, face to face – are preferable, but where proximity is felt to be too close it can be softened by an indirect orientation (that is, a turning away of the body to one side).

Bodily contact   In small, informal meetings, a touch on the arm can be reassuring and help to get a difficult point home. Or it may be easier to attract someone's attention. Handshakes at the beginnings and ends of meetings can be a small but very useful piece of body language.

Appearance and physique   People tend to give more attention to people who are taller. One easy way to appear taller in a meeting is to stand up to speak. As we said earlier, it may even assist audibility in meetings over a certain size. The clothes you wear can have a marked effect on how prepared people are to listen to you.

Timing and synchronisation   Dovetailing in discussions, identifying just the right moment at which to intervene and speaking for just the right length of time and no longer are techniques worth cultivating. As we said, much may be learned from observing others here. Don't be afraid of silences and pauses, they can be very useful in letting a point sink home.

Nonverbal aspects of speech   Listen to a sound or video recording of yourself speaking and you will be able to spot some of the things over which it may be worth exercising a little more control. Such things as the rate of speaking, speech errors (ers, ums and ahs, mispronunciations, etc.), tone of voice, pitch, volume can all be changed to suit the context in which the communication is taking place.

These, then, are some of the main points to bear in mind when seeking to improve your use of body language in meetings, whether as listener or as speaker. If you wish to delve a little deeper into this fascinating aspect of human communication, you may find it useful to read *Teach Yourself Body Language* by Gordon R. Wainwright (Hodder and Stoughton).

6

The Chair

Sometimes meetings are dominated by charismatic individuals who have nothing more to support their claim to pre-eminence than their ability to speak persuasively or their magnetic personality. More often than not, however, the most important and powerful person present is the chairman. He does not need a silver tongue or a compelling presence because the role he performs provides him with all he needs.

The position of chairman is the key one in any meeting. It is essential in all but the most informal and casual of meetings to have a chairman. He has at least five functions to fulfil:

(a) he must *preserve order* in the meeting, for without it no meeting can take place;
(b) he must be thoroughly familiar with and *enforce the rules of procedure* appropriate to the meeting;
(c) he must *rule on disputed matters* concerning procedure which arise during the meeting;
(d) he must *maintain the policy of the organisation* and draw members' attention to the fact if they are about to take a decision which conflicts with established policy; and
(e) he must *prevent irrelevant discussion* and keep the meeting to the agenda.

Sometimes, it will not be necessary to carry out these duties too rigorously, if at all. A chairman will rarely, for instance, have any serious problem in preserving order. Most of us are reasonable people and will be attending meetings from choice anyway, so we will have little cause to be disruptive on most occasions. In informal meetings, the rules of procedure may be largely ignored, if indeed any rules are set down for such meetings. Similarly, procedural disputes are unlikely in such meetings. And some meetings may actually encourage what appears to be irrelevant discussion if by doing so participants feel they have been able to get something off their chests.

A chairman can be a leader, guiding the discussion towards a decision which he has already determined upon. It is more usual, though, for a chairman to be impartial and not to take sides unless he has to. It is quite important to take the latter approach, for the chairman decides who speaks and in what order. If he favours one side too obviously, he is in for trouble, as many chairmen of local government committees find if they favour their own political colleagues too blatantly. Nothing is more likely to upset the opposition than to feel that they are being 'gagged', or prevented from speaking, by the chairman.

The chairman can vary the order of business, but he would normally be unwise to do so without the consent of the meeting. He has to remember that most of his authority stems from the meeting and that it can overturn his decisions if necessary. He would normally vacate the chair if that happened, at least for that meeting.

Personal qualities

Even though a meeting can, if it chooses, vote the chairman out of the chair, this is a rare occurrence and the chairman remains important to the success or otherwise of the meeting. He is the key person during the meeting and he needs to have certain qualities if he is to perform his duties properly. It helps if he is a calm and friendly kind of person who gets along well with most kinds of people. This is not to say that he should be the most popular person in the room. Popular people often do not have the necessary steel in their make-up to take people to task if they step too far out of line. A chairman must always be prepared to be a little unpopular if necessary, if others at the meeting are infringing the rules or not behaving in a reasonably civilised and acceptable manner.

A chairman should be clear thinking and not easily swayed by emotional or irrational considerations. He needs a level head if he is to advise a meeting on the best way of proceeding. This is especially true if the meeting contains opposing factions, as many political and local government meetings will.

Apart from knowing the rules, he needs a sense of humour. There is nothing worse than the pompous kind of chairman who is full of a sense of his own importance and who is not just serious but solemn as well. Many meetings benefit from an occasional light touch and a chairman who can provide it, without becoming too frivolous, is an asset indeed.

Above all, he has to be able to control his temper. Since it is not uncommon for debates in meetings to become quite heated, especially when people feel very strongly about issues, there has to be one person that the meeting can rely on not to be carried away by any tide of emotion. If a chairman loses his temper, a meeting is totally lost and in such circumstances it is perhaps best adjourned until everyone has had a chance to cool down.

It is important to remember the convention that all contributions in a meeting should be made 'through the chair'; that is, speakers preface their remarks with the words 'Mr Chairman . . .' or, if addressing another person directly, 'Through you, Mr Chairman, . . .'

When it comes to voting, the chairman usually has a vote like any other person present. It is also usual for him to have a casting vote which he only exercises if the votes for and against a motion are tied. If the chairman has not voted in the first vote, he cannot then exercise his own vote as well as his casting vote. It is also conventional that, regardless of the way he has voted the first time (if, indeed, he has voted), a chairman votes for the status quo (that is, the way things were before the vote was taken) and votes against the proposal. This avoids the often embarrassing situation of having decisions carried through on the chairman's casting vote. It has to be said, however, that this procedure is often ignored nowadays, particularly in political meetings. 'Hung' councils, where the parties are evenly represented, are often only able to transact business if the chairman casts his casting vote for his party's proposals. It is unsatisfactory, but it happens.

A chairman also needs to work very closely with the secretary of the organisation. We shall look at the secretary's role in more detail in the next chapter, but it is worth bearing in mind here that it is the secretary who does most of the work between meetings. If the chairman and the secretary do not have a close and amicable working relationship, then an organisation has many problems. In this respect, much will depend upon style of chairmanship.

Styles of chairmanship

There are many possibilities here and some are effective for some kinds of meetings, whilst others are better when the situation changes. If the main purpose of the meeting is to give or exchange information, an authoritarian style may well be appropriate. In this, the chairman gives a clear lead to the meeting, controls who is allowed to speak and stays very much at the centre of things.

If the meeting is seeking to make policy, the chairman may adopt a more consultative approach, still retaining enough control to avoid the meeting getting out of hand or spending too much time on less important aspects of policy. Some direction is called for, but members will need scope within the structure he imposes to say what they want to say in the way they want to say it.

If the meeting has been called to solve a problem, the chairman will probably wish to be more democratic and to allow a freer exchange of views in order to be sure that no possible solution is ignored. He will usually only need to exercise enough control to keep conflict within manageable proportions if there are factions supporting rival solutions.

In a meeting called to air grievances or to have some other kind of free-ranging discussion, the chairman may best operate as a facilitator, interfering as little as possible in the proceedings and giving most of his attention to making sure that all grievances are aired sufficiently or that all ideas are given voice. A permissive atmosphere is required, for very often the decision which is arrived at is less important than that it should be acceptable to as many as possible of those present.

It is neither possible nor desirable to specify which style of chairmanship is best in any given set of circumstances, but if a preference has to be expressed, it is perhaps to everyone's advantage if a chairman errs on the side of democracy and encouraging participation rather than on being too directive and authoritarian. In any event, a chairman's remarks to a meeting should be brief. No one goes to a meeting to sit and listen to a chairman telling them what to do, especially if he insists on doing it at length. That is a sure way to guarantee that no one turns up to the next meeting.

A good chairman will vary his style according to the purpose of the meeting and according to what he perceives to be the needs of those present. If there is a general rule, it is perhaps better to start off by being fairly strict and then to relax once it is clear that you have imposed your stamp upon the meeting. This may sound similar to the advice often given to teachers when taking a class for the first time. One would not want to equate a meeting of adults to a class of schoolchildren, but starting tough and then softening up is an approach which can work in a wide variety of situations. It is then easier to be tough if you have to be. If you begin soft, it is almost impossible to toughen up later. Many a teacher has found that out to his cost. It is also true that the greater the conflict in the meeting, the firmer the control needs to be.

Dealing with the hidden agenda

There is always a 'hidden' agenda and it contains the kinds of things listed in the table on page 16. The chairman's task is to detect what the items are on each occasion and decide what to do about them. He has basically two choices. He can ignore them and conduct the meeting as if they did not exist. He can recognise and accept their existence and bring them as fully out into the open as it is possible to do. People can be encouraged in such a way that they are given sufficient rope with which to hang themselves. For instance, if there is someone present whose inner wish is to work out his frustrations over a particular topic upon those present, the chairman may, by giving him free rein, create a situation in which those present react and in effect tell the person that they know what he is up to and that they will have none of it. Without having to do very much at all and by simply leaving it to those present, the chairman will have had at least one item taken off the hidden agenda. It is most unlikely ever to crop up again.

If two people are exhibiting signs of rivalry as part of their hidden agenda, an effective way of dealing with this is often to allow some time for the rivalry to surface and see if the meeting favours one approach or the other. If one person sees that he is on the losing side, this may well remove the rivalry from this particular arena. It may even remove it altogether. Very few people will pursue a course if they can see that they are gaining no support.

A similar result will often emerge if someone is using the meeting to seek increased status, perhaps by becoming regarded as the expert on a particular matter. If it is clear that others have similar claims to such status, the claim will be abandoned. Groups can have a powerful conditioning effect on individuals who seek to use the processes of meetings to satisfy personal objectives which are at variance with the group's wishes. A chairman may have to do very little in such circumstances other than to let the group make its feelings known.

Disruption

This can take many forms, from occasional sniping remarks to a refusal to obey a chairman's request that a speaker sit down and be quiet. Sometimes it is best to fight fire with fire and to be quite blunt in dealing with the disruption. On other occasions it may help to listen patiently to what the person causing the disruption has to say. Often, if such people feel that others have at least made a sincere attempt to understand their point of view, this will dissipate their aggression. It can also help for a chairman to restate what an objector has said, in an attempt to make it clear to the rest of the meeting just what he means. When people hear their viewpoint expressed in other words it can make them realise any weaknesses in their position or other deficiencies in their argument.

Occasionally in meetings these approaches will not work, perhaps because whoever is causing the disruption has determined to cause the meeting to break up. In this case a short adjournment often serves to defuse the situation and provide a cooling-off period in which people can make a more dispassionate assessment of their position. If this does not work, a chairman may have to abandon a meeting altogether and try to get the business done at another time. In a public meeting, he may even have to ask stewards to remove the offender or call the police to do this for him. Such action should be taken only as a last resort, for the feelings of bitterness which can be produced may sour an organisation's proceedings for months and even years.

Dealing with conflict

Conflict has many causes and not all of them will result in the kinds of disruption and aggression we have just been considering. Indeed, in meetings a certain amount of conflict is inevitable and even desirable. An organisation in which there is no conflict has no ideas. In many ways, it is not alive. Out of conflict can emerge a solution to a problem or a possible new course of action that otherwise simply would not be available to be taken.

Conflict has at least six main causes. It can be caused by being prevented from achieving something which is important to you. You may, for instance, be wanting to improve your working conditions as a result of the meeting. It can be caused by unpleasant conditions of another kind. For example, your boss may be making your life at work rather difficult and you may be trying to find some way of improving things through meeting and talking things over with colleagues.

Conflict may be caused because someone simply does not fit into a group. You may have someone in the team who is not pulling his weight and the meeting may be trying to find some way to a better response on their part. It may be the result of truculence against a 'foreigner'. There may be a new person in the office and a meeting may be necessary just to get people talking about the new situation this creates. There may be a small group within a larger group which is a source of conflict. Again, things may need to be talked over in a meeting. Or the conflict may be due to a good, old-fashioned communication failure. The meeting may be necessary to institute the kind of communication lines that will prevent such failures in the future.

There are other ways of resolving conflict and we can learn useful lessons from the ways in which different organisations and groups of people tackle the problem. The Quakers, for instance, have a quite unique approach. It may not be one which other organisations can practise very easily, but it is at least worth looking at. They insist on not making decisions until there emerges a unanimous view about what ought to be done. They have periods of silence after discussions so that matters can be considered carefully and dispassionately before a decision is taken. If a unanimous decision cannot be reached on a matter, they place a moratorium on discussing it (that is, they postpone a decision for a while and then try again to reach unanimity). They make sure that everyone present participates in the discussion. They learn to listen. They have no leaders or ranks, except for a chairman, so that no one is inhibited from expressing a view by considerations of status. And they keep the attendance at all meetings small in number. In these ways, the Quakers greatly increase the chances not only of arriving at sound decisions but also of arriving at decisions that everyone will support.

A scientific approach to the definition and analysis of problems can help to resolve conflict. Firstly, there needs to be a careful observation of all the facts. Secondly, a possible solution is proposed which is based upon the facts. Thirdly, the solution is tested, perhaps in a pilot project. Finally, action is taken as a result of the findings of the test application of the solution, with any modifications made necessary in the light of the experience gained.

If the conflict arises out of relationships between people, it can sometimes help if those involved role-play the situation, especially if in so doing they assume roles opposite to the ones they would play in real life. The insights gained by this can often be more far-reaching than helping to solve the immediate problem and may well result in permanent shifts in attitude which lead to a general improvement in working relationships.

Sometimes it simply helps if those involved in the conflict can be persuaded to pay more than usual attention to communicating clearly and simply with each other. If people can be trained to think, read, listen, speak and write more effectively, problems in communication, with the consequent generation of conflict, are less likely to arise.

Where conflict is inevitable it is perhaps best accepted and used. It can in fact be used, as we have seen, to allow people to let off steam. This is a valuable activity in itself and tends to make conflict a little less likely in the future. Nothing causes more unhealthy conflict than attempts to repress and bottle it up. This only stores trouble for the future. At least after an outburst, there is often a greater desire for peace and harmony than there was beforehand.

Controlling without controls

There are many advantages to reducing the role of the chairman and allowing a situation to develop in which meetings are controlled with a minimum of interference from the chair. This democratisation process means that others can express themselves more fully and freely. It works best if meetings are kept small and informal, but it can work with larger meetings. One way to reduce the power and authority of the chair (which is something that many people attending meetings can find quite intimidating) is to rotate the chair. This means that each person who attends a meeting has the opportunity over a period of time of being chairman. This has the additional benefit that it provides a kind of on-the-job training in chairmanship which not only improves everyone's skills but also makes them aware of the difficulties associated with chairing a meeting and the importance of having everyone co-operate with the chairman to see that the business proceeds smoothly.

It is quite possible for a chairman to deliberately hold back from stating his own views and expressly encourage others. It is also possible to allow the silences that inevitably occur during meetings to run their course. Many chairmen will feel that if everyone goes quiet then they must step in and get the discussion moving again. It may simply be that people need to pause a while and mull over what has already been said, or they may need time to assimilate a proposal which has just been made. Pauses and silences in meetings are not necessarily indications that everything that can be said has been said.

In many cases all a chairman really needs to do is to remind the meeting from time to time of the topic it is discussing, just to keep it on track. An agenda can sometimes be departed from, so long as the chairman keeps it in mind and brings the meeting back to it if in danger of straying too far. Above all, he needs to exercise tact in persuading people to keep to the point.

It can help if he allows the meeting to move quickly through routine and minor items and encourages it to dwell on the major ones. What he will have to watch is that it does not happen the other way round. We have all heard of tales of local government committees which have passed motions involving the expenditure of thousands of pounds 'on the nod' and have then spent thirty minutes discussing the merits and otherwise of spending a few hundred on repairing a public convenience.

One device to use with extreme care is the guillotine – that is, a pre-set time limit for the discussion of an item. This really needs the full support of a meeting to work well. If only one person feels aggrieved because of it, it may simply not be worthwhile in terms of the long-term resentment it will generate.

Reaching decisions

A chairman needs to be sensitive to signs that a meeting has discussed a matter for long enough and is about ready to make a decision. Sometimes this will emerge as a consensus because there are no more dissenting views and those which have been expressed are not being pushed. It may help at this point if the chairman summarises what he thinks the consensus is. If this meets with no opposition, the meeting should be able to move to a decision very quickly. If it is not agreed, it may be amended either by the chairman or perhaps by someone else present. In the event that a consensus cannot be reached a vote will usually be necessary, though votes should perhaps be avoided in informal meetings if possible.

In formal meetings, like those of local authority committees and many business board meetings, a vote may not only be necessary but desirable. With a vote, everyone can be clearer about what decision has been taken and exactly how much support it has. Votes can also be necessary when positions have become entrenched and, even though they know they have lost the argument, some people want their opposition to the decision recorded in some way. They can also be used by a chairman to cut short a lengthy and unproductive debate in which people have begun to repeat themselves and it is quite clear that a consensus will never emerge. There comes a point in such cases where a chairman has to say to himself that enough is enough and it is time for the meeting to move on to its next business or come to a close.

If a clear decision on a matter is required, it will also usually be useful to have a vote. In this way, people can see exactly how the matter stands. The less doubt there is after a decision the better. This is especially true where opinion is fairly evenly divided and the vote is close. Care must be taken on such occasions to count those for and against very carefully. If necessary, it is preferable to have two people counting independently. If they agree on the figures, there is less room for them to be disputed later.

The perfect chairman?

There is almost certainly no such thing as the perfect chairman, but perhaps we can detect something of a profile of the most desirable features of a good chairman from what has been said here.

A chairman should *vary his style* according to the purpose of the meeting, the people who are present and the kinds of matters to be discussed.

A chairman should *know what is on the 'hidden' agenda* and how to deal with the various items.

A chairman should *encourage people to speak* rather than try to rush the business through with a minimum of fuss and bother.

A chairman should be able to *deal firmly but tactfully and with humour with disruption* and aggression.

A chairman should be able to *use conflict productively* and to resolve it where it is not making a positive contribution to a meeting's proceedings.

A chairman should try where he can to *democratise* a meeting and only guide it when it is absolutely necessary.

A chairman should seek to *vary the pace* of a meeting, ensuring that most time is available to spend on the most important matters.

A chairman should *summarise the discussion* for those present at the meeting before proceeding to a decision.

A chairman should try where he can to *obtain a decision* from a meeting *without a vote* (unless a vote is necessary for the sake of clarity).

Above all, a chairman should *be thoroughly familiar with the rules* and procedures within which he has to work.

A chairman may not need to be perfect, but he needs sufficient mastery over the situation to be able to speak and act with authority when necessary.

7

The Secretary

If the chairman is the most important person during the meeting, the secretary is the most important person outside it. In many organisations, the chairman may have little or nothing else to do other than chair meetings. A secretary, on the other hand, has many things to do. Chairmen may come and go, especially if there are annual elections for the post. A secretary is much more likely to last, sometimes for many years. A full-time secretary may have a large number of tasks to perform between meetings.

In some organisations, like local authorities, those who act, in effect, as secretaries to meetings are known as *committee clerks* or *committee administrators*. They are the backbones of their organisations because almost all the business is conducted through meetings of one kind or another. This makes them indispensable to the efficient running of the various services and other activities. It is vital that such officers should have a sound grasp of the principles and techniques of committee administration and this chapter should be particularly useful to them, as it should for all those unsung heroes who keep the organisational wheels turning.

Even informal meetings can benefit by having someone fulfilling the role of secretary. It is always useful to have someone who will take minutes or at least some notes on what the meeting decided. It is useful to have someone who will take care of all the organisational aspects and make sure that there are no hitches like a double-booked room, no coffee available or people who do not turn up because they have not been informed about the meeting. And it is useful to have someone who can chase people up afterwards to ensure that action agreed is, in fact, done. For these and many other reasons, a secretary is an asset to almost any meeting.

It also helps if the secretary, like the chairman, possesses certain qualities, though these are not necessarily the same. The qualities needed in a secretary are:

(*a*)   he should be a good organiser;
(*b*)   he should be systematic in his approaches to tasks;
(*c*)   he should be stable and clear thinking;
(*d*)   he should be diplomatic;
(*e*)   he should be knowledgeable and authoritative.

Office organisation

Depending on the nature of the organisation and the secretary's precise role within it, he may well have to establish and maintain an office organisation, even if he is the only person in it.

Even a part-time secretary who has no office and works from his own kitchen table needs to have at least a minimal form of organisation. At the very least he will need the following items:

1   A file for letters he has to write.
2   A file for the business of each of the organisation's committees and sub-committees.
3   A file for previous correspondence.
4   A postage book.
5   A minute book or file for each committee and sub-committee.
6   An accounts book for petty cash, and a cash tin.
7   Items of office equipment, such as a typewriter, calculator and telephone.
8   A desk diary in which to record the dates of committee and sub-committee meetings and other relevant events.
9   All necessary items of stationery, such as letterheads, pens, pencils, paper clips, stapler and typewriter supplies.

In larger and more sophisticated organisations, the secretary may be a paid, full-time officer, as committee administrators in local government are. They have the full range of office facilities and equipment to call upon, but these office systems will still need to provide for the activities covered by the above list. In this way, routine tasks can be completed with a minimum of fuss and bother and the work of the organisation proceed smoothly.

In smaller organisations it is customary for the secretary to be an 'ex officio' member of all committees and sub-committees. That is, he is a member simply because he is the secretary. This ensures that there is always someone present who can take the minutes and ensure that decisions are carried out.

Constructing the agenda

The secretary or committee administrator has a great influence over what appears on the agenda for a meeting. He will usually draw up the first draft for the chairman to approve. On many occasions, the chairman will accept what the secretary suggests, unless he has an item or items which he particularly wants to have discussed, or unless he has a strong objection to an item the secretary has suggested putting to the meeting. If the relationship between the secretary and the chairman is of the kind it should be, such conflicts of opinion will be rare.

If both the secretary and the chairman dig their heels in over an item, with one wanting it to appear on the agenda and the other not, the matter can only be resolved by the meeting itself. In all matters of dispute between officers, the meeting they are servicing is the arbiter. In serious and long-running disputes, a special full meeting of the organisation may have to be called.

Most of the time, if not all the time, things like this simply will not happen, but it is no use thinking that disputes over the agenda, for instance, can be avoided by not having one. There has to be an agenda for all but the most informal and free-ranging of meetings, for at least three reasons:

1   It ensures that no item of importance is overlooked.
2   The business can be dealt with in a proper and appropriate order.
3   All members can be given proper warning of all items to be considered by the meeting, thus ensuring that things cannot be sprung on them without warning.

Even where the items on the agenda do not vary much from meeting to meeting, it is still preferable to have an agenda and for the secretary to ensure that the chairman reads it out to the meeting before proceeding to business.

As far as the order of items is concerned, a few general principles may be helpful. Minutes of the previous meeting and of committees or sub-committees which have taken place since the last meeting should be taken first. Major items will be taken next. This ensures that latecomers are likely to have arrived and early leavers will not have begun to depart. It thus ensures that important matters are discussed when there is the best chance of the maximum number of members being present.

Minor matters can then follow. These will usually be either non-controversial items, items requiring the expenditure of small amounts of money only, or items on which a report is to be called for so that it can be discussed at a future meeting. In meetings where members of the press or the general public are present, confidential items are best taken last. The usual procedure is to pass a resolution at the beginning of the meeting that the press and public are to be excluded after the last non-confidential item. It is common also to give the reasons for taking items in private, for example that it is to preserve commercial confidence (in the case of a company applying to a council for a loan) or it is to protect individuals (as when considering an employee's application for the regrading of his post).

Last of all comes 'Any Other Business' for those minor matters which do not have a place anywhere else on the agenda. Sometimes, as in many council meetings, there is no 'AOB'. Part of the reason for this is that it has been known for people to try to raise major items. It is part of the secretary's responsibility to ensure that his chairman does not fall into the trap of allowing this to happen. In fact, an important part of the secretary's job is to support the chairman and to guide him along the right path when necessary. This is not always an easy task, so it might be helpful if we take a closer look at this aspect of committee administration.

Influencing the chairman

The first task a secretary has in this respect is to *keep the chairman well informed*. Since it is normal for all incoming correspondence to be addressed to the secretary, there can be many matters that the chairman will not be aware of unless and until the secretary tells him. This gives the secretary considerable power and even more responsibility. A secretary only has to keep a letter to himself and he can have an influence not only over the chairman but over the organisation as a whole which extends to deciding which matters are discussed and which are not. This is a hazardous and deceitful route for a secretary to follow, however, for it only has to be discovered that he has been doing this and he will almost inevitably cease to be secretary of that organisation, and perhaps any other, for all time.

It is much better, both for the organisation and the secretary, if he is totally *open and honest with his chairman*. This does not mean that his power is diminished. If anything it is increased, because if the chairman agrees to the action the secretary would have taken on his own, the action has a firmer base. An organisation may disagree with and vote against a secretary who has taken action on his own. It is less likely to disagree with, much less vote against, the secretary and the chairman together. There is, after all, little point in electing people to senior positions which require them to exercise some kind of leadership and then refuse to follow them.

So the chairman should at least see all incoming information. It is best if he can have photocopies. Even in large organisations like local councils, where the chairman may only want to see major incoming information and leave routine stuff for officers to deal with, he should receive copies of such items.

A close relationship with the chairman is the key to having influence with the chairman. Let the chairman depend on you and develop a relationship of mutual trust and you can exercise your duties with a greater freedom and satisfaction. Where a chairman and a secretary or committee administrator do not trust each other, they have problems indeed. This is not to say that if, say, the chairman is an elected member and the secretary is a paid officer, the chairman lets the officer do everything and depends totally on him. Some chairmen may prefer to work this way, but many will not. But they should not go to the other extreme of distrusting everything the officer tries to tell them.

The chairman, as we have seen, rules on procedure during the meeting, but he may look to the secretary for advice. Some issues are clear cut and are easily resolved, but others may not be quite so straightforward and may depend upon interpretation. In such cases, a knowledgeable and authoritative secretary will be asked for an opinion. This raises the secretary's position and status within the organisation. The approach on such occasions should be flexible and should bear in mind that rules should be servants and not masters.

Secretarial roles

In addition to his role as the club, company or council organiser and chairman's right-hand man, the secretary has several other roles. He is, for instance, the committee's memory. It is he, after all, who writes the minutes. And he who writes the minutes in the first place is much more likely to remember them. This further enhances the secretary's stature and increases his importance in developing an effective organisation. He can further promote this himself by systematically keeping himself abreast of developments and keeping track of previous decisions so that he has a clear grasp not only of what is being enacted now, but also of how past actions have led to the present state of affairs. This enables him to make a vital contribution to the development of future policies and strategies. A secretary should keep a notebook in which he records details of things like problems discussed, solutions suggested, any other potentially useful ideas and of actions taken after meetings. This will provide him with information when it comes to writing minutes and it will also assist him in contributing to future developments.

The secretary is an important link person between the organisation and outsiders. As we have said, chairmen may come and go but secretaries usually last much longer. They thus provide stability and a continuing contact point that outsiders can refer to when they wish to know something about an organisation's activities. In local councils it may well be the elected members who make the majority of press statements, but in clubs and companies it is the secretary who often has to fulfil the role of media relations officer. We shall return to the question of the best approach to media relations in Chapter 9.

The secretary may even do more than liaise with the media and become a kind of ambassador for the organisation, going out and talking to other groups about what his club, company or council (or whatever it might be) does. Such activities can be very important when an organisation wants the public at large to have a favourable impression of it. Its image in the community will depend to a very large extent on how well the secretary performs this particular role.

Secretarial tasks

These roles imply a range of tasks for a secretary, but there are other tasks which are even more fundamental to his success as a secretary. As we have said, the secretary needs to be knowledgeable. He thus needs to brief himself before meetings even more carefully than other members. But there are other tasks, some of them quite mundane and seemingly trivial. If a secretary neglects them he undermines not only the organisation's effectiveness, but his own credibility as an efficient secretary. Some of the most common ones are listed for convenience in Figure 3.

Even before a meeting takes place, it is worth giving some thought to the form the minutes are going to take. We shall examine the task of writing the minutes in detail in the next chapter, because

Fig. 3 The secretary's tasks before the meeting

1 Briefing self on all matters which are known to be coming up or which are likely to come up at the meeting;
2 Drafting the notice convening the meeting and sending it out (sometimes this will go out at the same time as the papers for the meeting);
3 Constructing the agenda and consulting with the chairman and, perhaps, the vice-chairman over the items to be included, possibly at a pre-agenda meeting;
4 Circulating to the members of the committee, or other meeting, the relevant papers, including any necessary background information which needs to be included;
5 Listing all the items which it will be necessary to have to hand during the meeting in case a member asks a question or the secretary will need to refer to them for some other reason;
6 Contacting all the other people (council officers, company managers, club members and so on) who will need to be at the meeting to present reports or answer questions or fulfil some other function, to ensure that they will be in attendance;
7 Checking that the date and time for the meeting do not clash with any other meeting or event members will have to attend, that the room has been booked and all other necessary arrangements have been made.

accurate and concise minutes are essential to any organisation. But time can be saved later if the secretary prepares in advance a basic structure for the minutes which at least lists the agenda items in order and includes notes on what is likely to happen to each one.

Thought should also be given to the nature of actions which will have to be taken after the meeting and by whom. It will not be possible to be too specific at this stage and the list will have to be filled out and given flesh perhaps during the meeting and certainly afterwards. But it will still be useful for a secretary to have some early indication of the kind of workload that is likely to be generated. A list of the most common kinds of actions and post-meeting tasks a secretary may have to undertake is given in Figure 4.

Fig. 4 The secretary's tasks after the meeting

---

1 Writing the minutes of the meeting the same day (to ensure freshness of recollection) or as soon afterwards as practicable (in case of meetings which do not end until late in the evening) and either circulating them or placing them in the file of items for the next meeting (it is always desirable to begin to prepare for the next meeting as soon as the present one is over);
2 Conveying the decisions of the meeting to those who need to know them, particularly those who have been given tasks to complete (such as preparing reports) before the next meeting;
3 Ensuring that such people know exactly what it is that the meeting requires from them (this may require the secretary to expand upon and otherwise interpret the committee's wishes);
4 Listing all the other tasks to be performed as a result of the meeting in terms of:

   (a) memos to write to other people;
   (b) reports to be prepared;
   (c) telephone calls to make and to whom;
   (d) other meetings to be arranged of sub-committees or other groups of people;
   (e) any other action to be taken as a result of the meeting.

Secretarial problems

Most of the problems that arise during a meeting will be a matter for the chairman to resolve, but there are some that will either concern a secretary directly or which a good secretary can help to resolve. A secretary should not only seek to support the chairman where he can, in a matter like voting on the same side as the chairman (where the secretary does, in fact, have a vote), but should seek to support him in other ways.

If the chairman is new and inexperienced, he may have inadequate control over the meeting. A secretary can help such a chairman by talking over the procedure with him before the meeting and giving him some brief guidelines on what are likely to be the most difficult and controversial items. It is common, for instance, in local councils for the chairman and vice-chairman of a committee to have a pre-agenda meeting with the committee administrator and other relevant officers before the committee papers are sent out to the other members of the committee. At this meeting, the committee administrator can learn of the items with which the chairman, perhaps for political reasons, may have a problem and advise him accordingly on what he considers, in his professional opinion, to be the best approach.

If, during a meeting, it looks as if the decision which is going to be taken is an ill-considered one and the secretary or committee administrator knows that there is no political or other compelling reason why this should be so, he may suggest that it might be better to defer a decision, perhaps on the grounds that further information is needed about a specific aspect of the matter. This deferment will give him the chance to talk to the chairman and explain where the meeting was going wrong and why. On the next occasion when the matter is being discussed, there is then a better chance that the right decision will be taken.

If a meeting is rambling on and the chairman either seems unwilling or unable to keep it to the points at issue and make reasonable progress, a secretary may be able to tactfully take over some of the chairman's functions that the chairman is neglecting. He may, for instance, ask the chairman, ostensibly for the purpose of keeping the minutes straight, if he can summarise the situation as it appears to him. Periodic summaries are a useful technique for indicating to the meeting that they have completed one stage of the discussion process and are now ready to move on to the next.

If a meeting is passing resolutions which are vaguely expressed and possibly even contradictory, a secretary may be able to get the chairman to insist that motions are put into writing. A chairman can, after all, adjourn a meeting briefly in order to make time for this to be done. Written resolutions also have the advantage of making the secretary's task of writing the minutes easier.

If a meeting is but one in a series of meetings being held to consider a particular issue or problem, the secretary can help the chairman to keep a meeting on course and making steady progress if he offers a summary of the previous meeting(s). This helps the chairman to see ahead and keep track of what he has to do and, at the same time, establishes a frame of reference for the members to work within. The clearer the framework people are given in all kinds of contexts, and not just meetings, the more effectively they can operate.

Another problem a secretary may have is that he may not be able to provide the kind of advice and guidance that a meeting needs, because he simply is not sufficiently familiar with the law as it relates to meetings. In clubs and societies and other small and generally informal organisations, the number of occasions on which this kind of problem arises may be very small indeed. In companies, the chances are perhaps higher, especially in respect of formal business meetings like the annual general meeting of shareholders. In local government, it can be quite common that a member of a committee or the full council questions a decision or challenges a ruling and seeks an authoritative interpretation of one of the council's standing orders. In this last situation, the clerk to the meeting (who is fulfilling the role of secretary) has to be able to give such an interpretation and, for this reason, many chief executives of local authorities are persons who have had legal training. A secretary who has had no such training has to acquire it or at least learn enough about the law of meetings as he needs. Hopefully, the areas covered in this book will satisfy the needs of most secretaries in most organisations, but for those readers who need more than this, some of the books listed in the Further Reading section should be helpful.

More on local government

Committee administrators need to remember that the names of all members present must be recorded. Usually there will be an attendance book for members to sign. But the clerk will have to ensure that no member 'signs in' another member who has not yet arrived.

When votes are taken it will be the committee administrator's responsibility to count and record the votes for and against the proposition. Needless to say, such votes must be recorded accurately.

The committee administrator must be thoroughly familiar with the council's standing orders so that he can advise the chairman on procedure or if a member raises a matter relating to a particular standing order. Chairmen of such meetings are elected members and their grasp of standing orders is often sketchy to say the least. They should be familiar with them, but a committee administrator who relies on their knowing what they ought to know will soon find himself in difficulties.

Another factor committee administrators will need to watch concerns the minutes. Elected members, being politicians, sometimes say or decide things which they later regret and wish to change. The clerk must resist vigorously any attempt to change the nature of a decision after a meeting has taken place, in the same way that those who prepare Hansard, the verbatim record of the proceedings of Parliament, have to resist any attempt by a member to make changes in meaning, however slight, to what he said. Genuine mistakes and misunderstandings by the committee administrator are one thing, but attempts to make changes on any grounds other than inaccuracy must be rejected.

From time to time a member of a committee may seek guidance on whether or not he should declare an interest in a matter to be discussed. A member must make such a declaration if he or his wife has a pecuniary interest in any organisation with which the council is entering into a contract or is becoming connected in some other way. He must then not take part in any discussion or voting on the matter and may even have to leave the meeting during the discussion. Clearly, such a matter can become quite complicated and it is not possible to give a definitive ruling here. But the example does illustrate some of the problems a committee administrator may be faced with and the consequent need to be thoroughly familiar with his own council's provisions in such areas.

The roles of a secretary, then, can be many and varied. They can range from having to deal with the minutiae of planning and organisation to advising chairmen on abstruse points of law. Most of the time in most organisations he will be dealing with simple and straightforward matters in a systematic and purposeful way. But, as with any job, paid or voluntary, the unexpected can always happen. A good secretary at least prepares as best he can.

8

Writing the Minutes

The primary objective of minutes is to preserve a written record of the proceedings of meetings, whether they are general meetings, committee meetings or sub-committee meetings. They need to be accurate, clear and precise. They should record all motions put to a meeting, whether or not they have been passed, with a clear indication as to their acceptance or rejection. If a vote was taken, this too should be clearly recorded.

For meetings of directors or committees, the minutes should state who was present. For general meetings of members this is not necessary, except in the case of local authority meetings of the full council. Unless a clear-cut hierarchy exists, it is sensible to name the chairman first and list everyone else in alphabetical order.

The minutes must show exactly what has been decided. Where resolutions relate to expenditure, all details of amounts must be stated. Where resolutions have been amended, this must be shown precisely.

Minutes do not have to contain verbatim or even summarised accounts of what was said, though they may if an organisation prefers it this way. Since minutes are a record of what a meeting did rather than said, many organisations restrict them to decisions, plus the minimum necessary amount of explanatory information.

It should be remembered that it is always possible that the minutes may one day have to be produced in court to support a claim made by the organisation, or to defend one made against it. The outcome may depend upon the accuracy and completeness of the minutes with respect to decisions taken. If a decision is omitted, the court may infer that it was, in fact, never made.

The facts, then, which no minutes should omit are:

1 The date, place and time of the meeting.
2 The name of the chairman.
3 The names of those present (except for large general meetings).
4 The resolutions passed or rejected by the meeting.
5 The signature of the chairman (obtained at the next meeting when the minutes are approved) to indicate that they are a correct record.

If any person objects so strongly to a decision that he wishes his opposition to be recorded in the minutes, some organisations allow this to be done. Others do not.

When minutes are written, the various items require identification in some way so that matters can be referred to easily at a later date. One method is to number each paragraph in the minutes. Another is to number the resolutions. Either method can be used, but both are improved if the various agenda items are given appropriate headings to further assist identification and reference.

Again, when writing the minutes, the order of items should be the same as the order of items on the agenda. Minutes are not like a report of a meeting, where a writer can concentrate on what he thinks were the key items and ignore entirely matters which he thinks are of little importance. In minutes, every agenda item must be recorded and the decision made (or not made) recorded.

It can make the writing of minutes easier if, before a meeting takes place, the secretary (or whoever is taking the minutes) prepares an outline plan, using the agenda headings. Sometimes it will be possible to write the bulk of a minute beforehand, for example:

Chairman's Action – Application from —
The Chief Executive and County Clerk submitted a report (circulated) on the Chairman's approval of the purchase of a microcomputer plus ancillary equipment at a cost of £5122 for . . . This would be met from underspendings in the budget approved by the Committee for 19—/19—.

101 RESOLVED that the action of the Chairman be . . .

The minute can then be completed after the meeting by inserting 'noted' or 'confirmed' or even (if the chairman is unlucky) 'deplored' or 'not approved'. The meeting does not need to record any discussion that takes place, so there can be as little as a single word to be inserted to complete the minute. If a minutes writer can deal with only some of the minor items in this way, he will both save himself work after the meeting and be able to produce the minutes more quickly.

Despite being able to anticipate matters like this, it will be helpful to him if, during a meeting, the minutes writer makes more notes than he will actually require for the final draft of the minutes. This is especially true if it is the secretary who will have to write the minutes. It is always much easier to write something when you have more material to hand than you will need. As can be seen from the examples at the end of this chapter, minutes are written in a reasonably formal and impersonal style. They are written in the past tense. They should *never* be written in terms of 'we' or 'they'. The style has to appear objective and this cannot be done if the tone and style are too conversational and colloquial.

Unless a verbatim or word-for-word account is required, the minutes should err on the side of brevity rather than being too lengthy. But they must not be so short that someone reading them cannot understand what they are about, for example:

RESOLVED that IBB be requested to double the grant to NEDC.

Minutes are not always read only by those who attended the meeting and other readers may not be familiar with things like sets of initials. Writers of minutes in local government will need to bear in mind that they may be read by members of the general public who have a right to intelligible information.

At important meetings, such as annual general meetings or full council meetings in local authorities, it is desirable to have more than one person taking notes for the minutes. In this way, it is possible to cross-check afterwards to ensure accuracy and completeness.

Some organisations allow or require the chairman to vet the minutes before they are sent out. Where this happens, it has the advantage that the second opinion makes challenges to the minutes less likely at the next meeting. But it has the disadvantage that the chairman may be tempted to doctor the minutes to make the case of those whom he supports look a little more favourable than that of his opponents.

Sometimes, for very informal meetings or casual encounters of groups of people or meetings held over lunch or in some other semi-social context, minutes may not be necessary. They may not even be desirable, since some people feel unnecessarily pinned down if minutes are being taken. It may be better to have a 'note' of the meeting or some other form of report for the sake of future reference.

Figures 5 to 8 contain examples of minutes for various kinds of meetings. They should help you to see the range of approaches and styles within which minutes may be written. Groups or courses which are using this book as a text might like to discuss the relative merits of each.

Note: Minutes are normally numbered in sequence either from the beginning of the meeting (i.e. 1 to however many agenda items there are – say, 1 to 12) or from the beginning of the organisation's year (in which case, as in some of the following examples, the numbers can become quite high, but do provide for ease of reference over long periods of time). Sometimes it is agenda items which are numbered and sometimes it is the resolutions of decisions which are numbered. The choice is open to the organisation to select the method it finds most convenient.

Fig. 5   Minutes of a meeting of a board of directors – extract

A meeting of Directors was held at the Company's Offices on Friday 24 November 19—.

Present

Mr A. Brown (chairman)	Mr L. S. Lawrence
Mr R. Gordon	Mr E. Smith
Mr F. H. Hardcastle	Mr J. J. Johnson (by invitation)
Ms J. Hardy	

403   Minutes
Minutes of the meeting held on 23 October 19– (circulated) were confirmed and signed as a correct record.

404   Reports
The following reports were submitted to and approved by the Directors:

(a)   Personnel Ref. 342
(b)   Finance Ref. 77
(c)   Management Ref. 98
(d)   Sales Ref. 313
(e)   Research Ref. 187

405   The XYZ Co. Ltd
With reference to previous minutes about the proposed acquisition of The XYZ Co. Ltd, the Chairman referred to difficulties concerning the ownership of the Sunderland factory and the ownership of the land surrounding the factory.

Mr Gordon spoke of the problems which had arisen in relation to the ownership of the land and the fact that planning permission for the proposed developments had not yet been obtained. After a full discussion, it was decided that the negotiations be adjourned until counsel's opinion had been received.

406   Finance Report (Special)
Mr Lawrence presented figures relating to the Washington Project and requested urgent consideration to the question of approving a further allocation of finance.

Mr Gordon proposed, and was duly seconded, that the matter be referred to a special sub-committee of the Directors to report back to a full meeting in one week's time. The motion was defeated, there voting 2 directors in favour and 4 against.

After further discussion, it was decided to allocate a further £50 000, to be drawn from contingencies, to the Washington Project.

Fig. 6 Minutes of an Annual General Meeting of a voluntary organisation
– extract

FULWELL CHARITY ASSOCIATION

The Annual General Meeting of the Fulwell Charity Association was held at the Association's Clubhouse on Monday 13th May 19— at 6pm.

PRESENT

Executive Committee: Mr D. Evans (chairman), Mr T. Hodges, Mr L. Lowell, Mr G. Darlington, Mr N. Jay, Mrs I. T. Portman, Mr K. Long, Mrs W. Wilson, Mr P. White, Ms A. Dunn.
There were 39 members of the Association present.

APOLOGIES

Apologies for absence were received from Mr J. Jones and Mrs A. Brown.

FINANCIAL REPORT

The Hon. Treasurer reported on the Association's financial position (paper circulated). The report and accounts were adopted.

AUDITORS

It was agreed that Mr C. Green and Mr T. Young should be re-appointed as the Association's auditors for the ensuing year.

ANNUAL REPORT

The chairman submitted the annual report (previously circulated) for approval. The report was approved unanimously.

ELECTION OF OFFICERS

There being no nominations for officers, the present chairman, secretary, treasurer and executive committee were re-elected unanimously.

VOTE OF THANKS

A vote of thanks to the officers and the executive committee was proposed by Mr K. Long and seconded by Ms A. Dunn. It was carried unanimously.

Fig. 7   Minutes of a parent-teacher association.

SUNMOUTH SCHOOL
Parent Teacher Association

Minutes of a meeting of the Parent Teacher Association held in Room 3 on Monday 10 December 198–·

Present:

Mr C. Carson	Mr R. Goodman	Mr J. Fitzsimmon
Mr B. Shepe	Mr G. Simpkins	Miss J. Taylor
Mrs J. Robson	Mrs C. Simpkins	Mrs J. Holloway
Mr A. Beadle	Mrs A. Alderson	Mr J. Bird
Mrs M. Hutchinson	Mrs J. Smythe	Mr G. Johnson
Mrs A. Maiden	Mr J. Smythe	Miss B. Troon
Mr A. Watkinson	Mrs I. Macadam	Mrs J. Wheelwright

Apologies for absence

Apologies were received from Mr F. Emerson, Mr D. Dunn, Mrs C. Smith, Mrs J. Stopford.

1   Minutes

The Minutes of the previous meeting held on 12 November were taken as read.

2   Matters arising

School Newsletter: Mr Farrow is to attend our next meeting to furnish us with more information on the progress of this newsletter.

Minibus: Mr Dunn would like to pursue to possibility of hiring a minibus and has offered to gather further information for our next meeting.

PTA Newsletter: Mrs Wheelwright felt it would be a good idea to inform parents of the outcome of our fund raising efforts and she suggested a newsletter which could also be used to publish a list of committee members, which would be useful for parents.

Labelling: It was decided that Mrs Maiden be asked to order two dozen perspex labels and Mr Shepe be asked to order six brass plaques to be placed on the equipment the PTA has purchased.

3   Correspondence

A letter of thanks was received from Mr Fitzsimmon for our allocation to his computer fund. Mr Dunn also sent his thanks for our help.

A request for a donation to St George's Fire Appeal Fund was received from J. Blyton and it was decided to send a contribution of £20 on behalf of the PTA.

4   Calendar of events

Mr Shepe suggested that everyone should make a list of events they would think interesting. It was suggested that a diary of events be pencilled in for the year. Further details and precise dates could be finalised later.

January: Microwave demonstration. Mrs Maiden agreed to make further enquiries and, if possible, it was hoped that Mr Smythe would be able to obtain raffle prizes.

February: Darts and Dominoes evening. This would have a pea and pie supper included and a suggested venue was the Rotunda at the school with a Rent-a-bar. J. Fitzsimmon agreed to organise the darts matches. Mrs Wheelwright and Mrs Simpkins would organise the domino games.

March: Spring Fling – Ceilidh
         Beetle Drive – Pie and Pea Supper
         Car Boot Sale

April: Quiz

May/June: A day at the Races.
         Summer Fayre. A sub-committee was formed to organise this. The members are: Mrs Simpkins, Mrs Wheelwright, Mrs Robson, Mr Watkinson and Mr Goodman.

5 Federation Report

There was no report this month.

6 Any other business

Cross Country: Mr Shepe again raised the question of unsupervised cross-country runs. Mr Carson said that a report was in progress but because of recent industrial action by the teachers this had been delayed. The local authority did not intend to propose a policy but cross-country running was not to be encouraged.

Detention: Mrs Alderson asked if 24 hours' notice was school policy for detentions. Mr Carson said that it was a school rule and unless special arrangements had been made must be strictly adhered to. If a parent refused to allow detention, that parent would be contacted and asked to call at the school.

7 Date of next meeting

The next meeting would be held on Monday 14 January 198– at the school in Room 3 at 7.15pm.

There being no further business, the meeting closed at 9.05pm with the Chairman wishing everyone the compliments of the season.

Fig. 8   Minutes of a local government meeting – extract

Bartonshire County Council
Minutes of Economic Development Committee
3 April 198–

Present   Councillor Wainwright in the Chair.
Councillors Avon, Connors T., Cousins, Cranner, Davis, Fearns, Fitz-william, Gillespie, Gray, Hammer, Hilton, Hodges, Jefferson, Kirkby, Lane, Lewis, McKinroe, Martin, Murray, O'Shea, Pearson, Rudham, Smythe-Holme, Spears, Taylor, Turnball and West.

Co-opted members
Councillors Murphy (N. Barton) and Tait (W. Barton).

Apologies
Councillors Moore and Marshalls.

Minutes
183   RESOLVED that the Minutes of the Meeting (circulated) of 23 March 198– be confirmed and signed as a correct record.

Energy sub-committee
184   RESOLVED that the Minutes of the Meeting (circulated) of 28 March 198– be noted and the following be approved:

(*a*)   C.H.P. for West Barton: Resolution 40(*a*)
that the Association Heads of Agreement dated 6 August 198– be terminated so far as the County Council is concerned, and,
(*b*)   *Anti-PWR Consortium*
that a grant of £75 be made to the Anti-PWR Consortium to make up their budget deficit.

Joint Economic Development Planning sub-committee
185   RESOLVED that:

(*a*)   the Minutes of the Meetings (circulated) held on 14 and 20 March 198– be noted, and,
(*b*)   the County Planner be requested to report on the progress of the South Sands reclamation scheme.

Training sub-committee
186   RESOLVED that the Minutes of the Meeting (circulated) of 22 March 198– be noted.

Promotions sub-committee
187   RESOLVED that the Minutes of the Meeting (circulated) of 22 March 198– be noted.

Media Development Working Group
188   RESOLVED that the Minutes of the Meetings of 15 and 29 March

198– (circulated at the Meeting) be noted, and the following recommendations be approved:

(a) a training facility for the provision of a basic rehearsal studio (as detailed on the attached Plan) be incorporated in the Brookfield Complex;

(b) the County Architect be authorised to produce a detailed design for the structural alterations and service supply for the project;

(c) the Officers and NBDC discuss as a matter of urgency the specialist fixtures and fittings, equipment and running costs for such training scheme; and

(d) the Media Development Group be authorised to examine and report on (c) above and report thereon to the Committee.

East Bartonshire Conference at Oldcastle University, Birmingham

The Chief Executive and County Clerk submitted a report (circulated) on a conference on poverty which was to be held at Oldcastle University on 25–26 April 198–· As it was not on the list of authorised conferences, approval would be required from Policy and Resources Committee.

189 RESOLVED that:

(a) approval for the above conference be sought from Policy and Resources Committee, and

(b) four Councillors from the Conference Rota be authorised to attend.

Appointment to Bartonshire Microsystems Centre

Councillor Gillespie informed the Committee that he had previously been appointed as the County Council representative to the Bartonshire Microsystems Centre but that he had found it difficult to attend meetings and wished to resign. Furthermore he felt that it would be more appropriate to appoint an officer as a representative as there were no other elected members sitting on the Board.

190 RESOLVED that Councillor Gillespie's resignation from the Bartonshire Microsystems Centre Board be accepted and that the Chief Executive be appointed to serve on the Board of the Centre and he be requested to submit regular progress reports to the Committee.

TUC Construction Industry Bulletin

The Chief Executive and County Clerk submitted (circulated) for information a copy of the TUC Construction Industry Bulletin No. 8.

191 RESOLVED that the Bulletin be noted.

Action Programme for Jobs and the Environment

The Chief Executive and County Planner submitted a report (circulated) and the above document produced by East Bartonshire MBC, which set out a number of priority measures aimed at the economic problems of the area.

192   RESOLVED that:

(*a*)   the case for greater Government financial input to back up local initiatives as put forward in the East Bartonshire report be supported, and

(*b*)   the report of the Chief Executive and County Clerk be approved as the County Council's response on the economic development initiatives referred to in the East Bartonshire report.

The future of the coal industry
The Chief Executive and County Clerk submitted a report (circulated) which dealt with two issues relating to the coal industry as follows:

A   *The Future of the Westerland and Scarvale Coalfield*
The Trade Union Studies Information Unit had been commissioned to produce an economic and social audit into the effects of the run-down in the mining industry. This was attached to the report for members' comments.

193   RESOLVED that:

(*a*)   the report prepared by TUSIU on the situation in the mining industry be approved and authorisation be given to the publication of the Report on a low cost basis;

(*b*)   TUSIU be requested to produce a summary of the report which would highlight aspects of concern and which could be given a wider circulation, and

(*c*)   Scarvale County Council's views on the document be sought and they be invited to participate in funding the cost of publication.

B   *Coalfield Communities Campaign*
A letter had been received from Brindsley MBC requesting the County Council to consider participating in the Coalfield Communities Campaign. A regional meeting was to be held at Burnside Borough Council on 27 April 198– to which the County Council was invited to send a representative.

194   RESOLVED that:

(*a*)   the County Council participate in the Coalfield Communities Campaign, and a contribution of £500 be made towards the expenses of the National Campaign; and

(*b*)   Councillor Smythe-Holme be appointed to represent the County Council in both local and national aspects of the Campaign and associated activities.

9

Action After a Meeting

Once a meeting has ended, the general expectation is that those who attended will go away and do the things the meeting agreed they should do. Life, however, is not always like that. People may leave a meeting with the best of intentions and then find that something else happens to distract their attention from the matters dealt with during the meeting. This then becomes the new priority. If this kind of thing gets out of hand, it may lead to a situation in which nothing ever gets done because people simply do not follow up what was decided at the meeting.

What is needed is some kind of procedure for ensuring that meetings do not become irrelevant because people just do not take them seriously enough. What is needed is a system of checks and safeguards to make sure that action takes place. Very often it is the secretary who is responsible for chasing people up. But the real responsibility falls more widely than that. *Everybody who attends a meeting has a responsibility to see that it succeeds.* The kinds of points which need to be considered are listed in Figure 9. Most of these are points which the secretary will take care of, but he is more likely to take care of them if he knows that the other people who were present will be looking at the list. Those whose job it is to chase us may be more inclined to do that if they know that we shall chase them if they don't.

It can help for someone in the organisation to take a close look at the meetings which are held, to see if any of them are redundant or lacking in purpose. Again, it may be the secretary who does this, but it can be beneficial if it is done by somebody who is not normally

Fig. 9　Action after a meeting

A checklist

1　First draft of minutes to be prepared as soon after the end of the first meeting as possible (preferably the same day, but certainly within 48 hours).

2　Action sheet (see Fig. 12 on page 100) for who has to do what, how and by when, or leave a column at the side of the minutes with the appropriate name written next to each action that has to be taken.

3　Someone to check that action has been taken, usually the secretary or committee administrator, or one of his assistants.

4　Any meetings requested to be arranged as soon as possible and the appropriate people informed.

5　Anyone who needs to know to be told what decisions were made at the meeting, perhaps by making sure they receive a copy of the minutes.

6　A personal checklist (the action sheet in Fig. 12 can also be used for this purpose) of the things that you have to do before the next meeting.

7　Draft minutes to be checked by the chairman before final typing (if this is, indeed, the organisation's practice).

8　Typed minutes to be kept in appropriate files. All members of a committee should consider keeping their own files, at least for the last six months, for, even if there is a library where they are kept, it aids ease of reference for future meetings where the same topics may rear their heads again.

9　Check for any other action that needs to be taken.

heavily involved in meetings. They may be able to take a more dispassionate and objective view. It may even be better, if the finance is available, to call in an outside consultant to review the meetings process and perform a committee inventory or audit. Once someone comes around and asks 'Why is this meeting taking place?', it can concentrate the mind wonderfully. Organisations are always prone to continue doing things long after the original point and purpose has disappeared. (See also Chapter 14.)

If committees are found to be unnecessary they should be abolished, or at the very least have their terms of reference reviewed and redrawn. A committee may be given a new lease of life in this way. More often, though, it will be desirable to be ruthless and chop a committee out of the meetings cycle. Since, in the modern organisation, meetings seem to reproduce themselves too easily, it does no harm to try to reduce their number whenever the opportunity presents itself.

Informing others

Telling others about what has happened at a meeting need not be simply restricted to those who are directly affected by it or who will have some work to do as a result. Depending upon the context, it may even involve informing all the people who work for an organisation or even the public at large.

Even if the people to be told are small in number (say, the other managers in an organisation), the information will almost certainly be better conveyed in writing rather than orally. This helps a communication system to be established and removes the doubt – or most of it, for no system is infallible – about whether or not some-one has been told. In the case of many voluntary organisations, however, because finance is limited and people are probably working part-time, the communication will have to be oral.

Sometimes it is more effective, if the numbers of people who have to be told are large, to produce a bulletin or newsletter. This usually then makes it possible to tell people about all sorts of things which they might not otherwise find out about. They can also be encour-aged to use it themselves if they wish to communicate to the rest of the members of the organisation.

Whatever method is used, it is beneficial to an organisation if information circulates reasonably freely within it. Much less conflict and disruption is likely to be caused where people know what is going on than where they do not.

When it comes to communicating information about meetings to people outside the organisation, the problem becomes much more complex, and much more sophisticated (and expensive) methods may need to be employed. The techniques of advertising, public relations and media relations become useful. Councils now have a duty to keep the public informed of their activities and many other large organisations will also find it desirable on a number of counts. It helps to improve the organisation's image, make it more highly regarded, soften any possible public criticism of its activities, and generally help it to demonstrate that it serves a useful function in society.

Large organisations may even employ specialists in these areas, either on the staff or as consultants. The secretary should have ready access to them if this is the case. But other members of a meeting may be asked for their views or comments and the more experienced they become at doing this, the better the organisation will be served. Good communications externally are at least as important as good communications internally.

Even small organisations, like local clubs and societies, will find it beneficial to foster good public relations. It need not be expensive. Often local newspapers are more than pleased to carry details of meetings. It all helps them to sell copies, because it is a part of their task of keeping people informed about what is going on in the town, city or country area which they serve.

There is a good case, then, for any organisation which holds meetings to have a public relations officer. It may be someone appointed specifically for that purpose, or it may be the chairman or the secretary or even a small sub-committee. Whoever is charged with the task, they should consider at least three methods of disseminating information without incurring great cost:

1 Personal contact with people outside, either by word of mouth or by giving talks to other local organisations and the like.

2 A simple newsletter or bulletin which appears at regular intervals (regularity is more important than frequency, because after a time people begin to expect and even look forward to its appearance).

3 Media relations – making sure that information is passed on to the local press (including 'freesheets'), local radio, regional television (who may only be interested in major events, national prizes won by local individuals or organisations doing things which no organisation has done before – TV is nearly always interested in 'firsts'), and journals and magazines (it is often easier to get information into professional and technical or trade journals than into the other channels of communication listed above).

An organisation entering for the first time into this area of activity will find it useful to carry out a systematic survey of the possibilities that exist for publicising its activities. It can help to begin by looking at what other organisations are doing and the following steps may be worth following:

1 Make a list of all relevant newspapers. Do not neglect 'freesheets', the local newspapers which are distributed free

because they are paid for by advertising. These often contain quite substantial amounts of editorial material and, because they usually have skeleton staffs, they tend to be on the look-out for interesting copy.

2   Make a list of the magazines and journals which are popular in the area to be covered.

3   Make a list of any other relevant publications. Do not neglect seemingly unimportant publications like church newsletters, parish magazines, trade union publications or the supplements sometimes inserted monthly in the local paper by local councils, for they will often carry information about the activities of others in their areas.

4   Make a list of all the radio and television stations which cover your area and of the programmes which are likely to take outside information.

5   Study the above to see what information they contain over, say, a four-week period about organisations like your own.

6   Assess how they have used the information that has, clearly, been passed on to them.

7   Make a list of contact persons – one for each – who can be telephoned or written to when necessary. If no name is immediately obvious, telephone them and ask whom you should send your information to. They are almost certain to be helpful because they cannot exist without a good and continuing supply of information.

8   Plan your strategy. Which will you send material to first? What kind of information is most likely to be accepted by each? Will you need photographs? Will you need to make provision for television cameras? Are there any who will only respond if the information is 'exclusive' (i.e. no one else receives it)? And so on.

9   Put your plan into effect and begin to send material out.

10 After three months review your success and adapt your approach to improve it and make it even more successful.

In addition to all of this externally directed work, there will be other tasks which someone will need to perform. Often it will be the secretary, but it could involve others.

Filing and checking

Once the minutes have been written, someone will need to check their accuracy. Clearly, the person who writes them will do this, but it can be helpful if someone else does it, too. A second opinion can be most useful in spotting errors which the person who has actually written the minutes has overlooked because he has read them as saying what he expected them to say. An outsider will be conditioned by no such preconceptions.

Minutes and papers will need to be filed. This is necessary if they are to be available for easy reference in the future. Different organisations use different methods, but some of the more common ones are:

1   According to committee;
2   According to topic;
3   Alphabetically;
4   Chronologically.

In a sense it does not matter too much which system is chosen, so long as it meets the needs of the organisation and that it is kept to. The main requirement, then, is for a system. *Which* system is chosen is a little less important.

As a result of the meeting, there will be memos and letters and reports to be written. Chapter 13 deals in some detail with the writing of reports to be presented to committees and other groups, because this is a very important part of the meetings process. No less important but perhaps a trifle easier to deal with are memos and letters. Much of what is said in relation to the writing of reports will also apply to other forms of written communication (and, indeed, to any form of communication), but Figure 10 offers some specific advice about writing memos. To make the point a little more effectively, the advice is given in memo form. Figure 11 does the same sort of thing for letter writing. Hopefully, these two demonstrations will be of use to a wide range of readers. Those who require more extended treatment of this aspect of committee and group work will find some of the titles in the Further Reading section helpful.

Fig. 10

To:	Readers	*Date:* 21/6/—
From:	Gordon Wainwright	*Ref:* GRW/JG

Subject: MEMO WRITING

Memos should:

1 Be as brief as possible and aim for accuracy, clarity, conciseness and simplicity;
2 Deal with a single subject;
3 Request or give specific information or guidance, or call for specific action or response;
4 State any deadline clearly;
5 Be dated;
6 Give a reference identification;
7 State the subject clearly and concisely;
8 Try to be positive rather than negative;
9 Make use of subtitles in those longer than one page;
10 Only be used if it is necessary to have a written record of what you have said. Face-to-face communication is more effective;
11 Indicate the degree of urgency for any action required;
12 Use short, numbered paragraphs or statements;
13 Be sent only to people who really need them.

The next meeting

There is a great temptation to see meetings as separate events and, of course, in a sense they are. But it is important to regard them as part of an ongoing process. They are a vital part of the way any organisation conducts its affairs. As soon as one meeting finishes, the next one can be said to have begun because the work that is carried out after a meeting has finished will almost certainly be reported on and the only place this can really be done is at the next meeting.

Meetings can, therefore, become self-perpetuating institutions and each one contains the seeds of its successor. Perhaps this is one of the reasons why there are so many meetings and why they seem to crop up with ever-increasing frequency. We shall return in Chapter 14 to the need to keep a careful eye on this process and to explore the possibilities that exist for using alternatives to meetings.

It is also important to appreciate how meetings integrate with the rest of the work that an organisation does. In business and industry, for instance, meetings are usually intended to lead to changes,

Fig. 11

GRANGETOWN BOROUGH COUNCIL
Civic Centre
Grangetown GN1 1AA
Telephone: 799799

Please reply to:　G. R. Wainwright　　　　　　　　　　　　　　Ext: 105

21 June 19—

Course Members
Committee Administrators' Course
Wearside College
Sunderland SR2 9LH

Dear Course Member

LETTER WRITING

The basic rules of accuracy, clarity, conciseness and simplicity apply to letter writing as much as to any other kind of writing. In letters to the general public, they apply even more strongly. Letters which deal with problems, as opposed to simply giving or requesting information, should be especially carefully written to avoid possible misinterpretation.

In addition to general rules of written expression, some more specific rules apply:

1　Follow the standard conventions in the writing of official/business letters;
2　Pay particular attention to layout;
3　Be courteous and tactful in expression;
4　Match the valediction to the salutation (that is, 'Yours faithfully' goes with 'Dear Sir' and 'Yours sincerely' with 'Dear Mr . . .');
5　Avoid archaic or flowery expressions;
6　Use personal pronouns where possible;
7　Avoid long, formal words;
8　Start with the important point;
9　Keep letters to one page wherever possible. If longer, consider using sub-headings;
10　Be careful over the tone of the letter;
11　Always check dictated letters particularly carefully;
12　If you are dictating a letter, work from a plan, dictate slowly, keep sentences short and avoid repetition;
13　Try to specify dates and actions where relevant;

14 Pay particular attention to opening and closing sentences;
15 Avoid slang expressions and clichés;
16 Reply to letters promptly.

You should remember also that the general principles of preparation, assessment, planning, expression and review apply as much to letter writing as they do to reports, memos, articles, books and all other forms of writing (see Chapter 13 in this book).

Yours sincerely

Gordon Wainwright

Gordon Wainwright
Chief Executive

---

preferably improvements, in the work situation. It may be that as a result new targets are set for the performance of individuals or groups, or it may simply be that they are given specific tasks to perform. It is necessary, therefore, as part of the process of post-meeting checking, in this context, to ensure that certain questions are satisfactorily answered:

1 If the meeting was dealing with a problem, was a solution found?
2 Was the solution a complete answer or does further work still need to be done?
3 Have there been any unforeseen consequences of the solution?
4 Does anything specific need to be done to take account of this possibility?
5 Were any special tasks to be performed by individuals or groups carried out as expected?
6 If not, what other action needs to be taken?
7 Have the meeting and its consequences been effectively integrated into the organisation's operations as a whole?
8 If not, does any special action need to be taken?
9 Have any circumstances arisen which may justify the calling of a special meeting before the next scheduled meeting?
10 Are there any other factors which need to be taken into consideration or acted upon?

Fig. 12

Post-Meeting Action Sheet

Details of meeting: committee/sub-committee/other:

Date: Chairman:
Time started: Present:
Time finished:
Place:

Agenda Item	Brief Description	Decision	Action Required	By Whom	By when	Action completed √ or X

10

Particular Kinds of Meetings

So far we have been considering meetings and committee procedure from a broadly general point of view, although we have used examples to illustrate specific points from time to time. Now, however, it will be helpful if we focus clearly on particular kinds of meetings and see how the general principles apply to them. This will enable us to see both the similarities and the differences which exist. It will also enable the reader to learn more about those kinds of meetings in which he is interested. For this reason, the headings in the chapter relate to the kind of meeting being discussed in each case and the reader may choose to ignore those meetings which do not feature in his present or likely future experience. Naturally, for those who are prepared to take the time, there are useful lessons to be learned even from those meetings with which one is not directly concerned.

This survey of practice in particular kinds of meetings will also serve to show that the procedure for conducting meetings often needs to be applied flexibly if it is to work. Rules and conventions are always very useful in helping us to work purposefully and systematically, but there is no sense in following rules simply for the sake of following them. The main thing, as in many other kinds of activities, is to know when you are breaking a rule and to know that in doing so you will achieve a better result than you can by following the rule.

Formal meetings (e.g. Council)

One purpose council meetings have which other meetings do not is to provide a *public and democratic forum* in which decisions can be made. There is a set agenda which is usually published a week or so before the meeting. In addition to being circulated to councillors, it will also be sent to the press and to other individuals and organisations who have requested it. In the last case, it may be sent out without confidential items and other reports on which members have not yet made a decision. The meetings will usually be large. Councils of more than sixty members are not uncommon. The meeting will be held in a specially constructed council chamber and it may be that few, if any, other meetings are held in that room. There is often a time limit specified for council meetings in standing orders. When that time is reached, the council either adjourns to the same day and time in the following week or the members may vote to *suspend standing orders* and carry on until the business is finished.

Councillors should be especially careful to brief themselves properly on the matters to be discussed at the meeting. They are elected representatives of the people and are responsible for spending large amounts of other people's money. This is not a task to be undertaken lightly. Since the electorate may wish to know whether or not their local councillor was present at the meeting, it is more than usually important that apologies for absence are notified in advance. Lobbying is a common activity before meetings, especially if the balance of the parties is a fine one or if there is no party whip imposed upon an issue.

During the meeting, the chairman (or mayor, as he or she is sometimes called) will work quite briskly through the agenda, keeping to the order of items as detailed in the council summons (the notice convening the meeting). Rules of debate will be spelled out in some detail in the council's standing orders and will cover such things as the time limit upon speeches, a provision that a person may only speak once on a matter, the circumstances under which a speaker has a right of reply, and so on. Motions will be printed and, except for procedural motions, no motions will be accepted during the meeting. Points of order will be dealt with straight away, as they take precedence over all other matters. There will be a specified quorum and no business will take place if the required number of members is not present. Decisions will be reached by vote, usually by show of hands, but sometimes by named vote, in which each member's name is called out by the clerk (that is, usually, the chief executive of the council) and he replies 'For' or 'Against'.

Participation in debates in formal council meetings is often limited to the key speakers on each side. The event is to some extent stage-managed. Members of the public who go to watch their local council meeting from the public gallery should not be surprised if their local councillor never opens his mouth. He will have had his say when the issues were on their way through committee and sub-committee.

The chair will always be taken by the person elected as chairman or mayor for that year (or the deputy chairman or deputy mayor) and the secretary will be the chief executive (or town clerk or county clerk as he is sometimes called). The clerk will advise the chair quite strongly, if need be, on any points of procedure or law which arise. The minutes will be taken by two of the committee administrators in considerable detail, but when the minutes are published they will often contain only the decisions made, together with any necessary explanatory information. The press will be present at the meeting and the council's press officer will be at pains to try to obtain from them favourable coverage of the council's activities.

Formal committees (e.g. Council committees)

Similar provisions will apply as to full council meetings, but the rules are not usually applied quite so strictly. For instance, written notice usually has to be given to ask a question in council, but this rule will not be applied in committees. Once again, there will be a set agenda. The size of the committee will be between twenty and forty members if it is a main committee, about ten to twenty if it is a sub-committee. There will not usually be a time limit set for the meeting, but most will last less than two hours.

The proceedings will be similar to those for full council meetings, but adapted to meet the committee situation. The chairman will work through the agenda, but will be less inflexible when it comes to varying the order of items on the agenda. He may also be more willing to let people speak more than once on a matter. There will not necessarily be a vote to record decisions unless those who are opposed to a proposal wish to press their opposition to a vote.

Participation will generally be freer, although all remarks will still be addressed 'through the chair'. The committee administrator will be more likely to be asked whether an action is within the committee's powers and terms of reference than to give advice on a procedural ruling. This is because the approach in committees is more positive: more of a council's real work is done by committees and sub-committees than by the full council. Many authorities delegate considerable powers to committees and these may often not need to go to council for approval.

Informal committees

In many organisations, informal committees are established to examine a problem or oversee a function. In such committees, the adherence to the rules of committee procedure is even less strict. There may be no written agenda, but simply a list of topics which the chairman has and which he reads out before the meeting begins. The number in attendance will usually be less than a dozen. The location may be in a committee or board room, but it could just as easily be in someone's office. There will not normally be a pre-set time limit, though it is not at all a bad idea to agree a finishing time in advance. It concentrates people's minds and makes them realise that they are there to do business and not merely act as a talking shop. Apologies for absence may or may not be given. There will be little lobbying in advance because people will not yet have reached a position on many of the issues where they can be persuaded to make up their minds.

The meeting may work quite loosely through the agenda, returning to an item if it chooses or if someone has second thoughts. There will be no such things as rules of debate, motions, points of order, or the like. A quorum may be as little as two people, or even one. Decisions will be reached by consensus more often than not. Participation will be encouraged. There may be no formal secretary, but someone will prepare an action sheet and be delegated to chase it up to make sure things get done.

Working parties and discussions

Here, the rules relax even further and there may not even be a chairman. There may be no agenda other than a topic to discuss. The number attending will be kept as low as possible, say somewhere between three and ten. The location can be a room almost anywhere – even a quiet lounge in a local pub – and there will be no time limit other than the willingness of the participants to stay on. Advance briefing may be quite detailed, depending upon the topic for discussion, but members will normally be expected to have done a fair amount of research before they arrive. Apologies for absence are not usually necessary, but still (as always) remain a courtesy, and there is no need for any lobbying since the discussion of the topic will be in its infancy. There will rarely be an agenda, and a minimum of procedural rules. Normal courtesies of civilised conversation will be enough.

Everybody is encouraged to participate as fully as possible. There may or may not be a chairman and secretary, but these roles may usefully be filled whatever the meeting. No minutes will be produced, but there may be a 'note' of the meeting prepared. There will be no formal communication to others outside the working party until such time as it feels it has reached its conclusions.

Negotiations (business)

There may be no agenda as such but everyone will know what he wants to talk about, at least in general terms in the early stages. The numbers present will preferably be small, perhaps no more than two or three. The location will usually be someone's office but it could just as easily be a restaurant or someone's hotel suite. The duration will not be pre-set, but will be limited by the fact that everybody will have other business to do with other people elsewhere. Those who are trying to sell or persuade will have to be especially well briefed; those who are being sold or persuaded will at least need to have a very clear idea of their requirements, to avoid being sold something which will not meet their needs or being persuaded to accept something they should question.

There will be no agenda, or even if there is it will change as the meeting proceeds. Formalities, if present, will be of a different order and related perhaps to cultural differences in approach, if the participants come from different countries. Not everyone may participate, but only those who have been designated to speak or who are asked a specific question. In fact, one or two experts – legal, financial or technical – may be there just in case they are needed.

There will be no chairman, but a kind of joint chairmanship by the leaders of each side. There will be no secretary, but a shorthand taker may be present to record what is said. There will be no minutes, but a 'note' may be agreed of the main points covered.

Negotiations (industrial relations)

There will usually be an agenda agreed for such meetings, because each side will need to prepare in advance by collecting facts and figures and other information. The numbers may be small. If they are large – if, say, a whole union executive committee has to be present – they will not be so useful. Location will normally be a board room, but could be someone's office. The meeting will have a chairman, who will normally be the senior person present on the management side. The proceedings may not follow rules of debate or other procedures, but will have to be reasonably systematic and smooth running. Letting people speak only once, and similar rules, are highly unlikely to work in this kind of context.

One thing which needs to be watched particularly carefully is the seating arrangement in the room. It is important to avoid patterns that will too easily lead to confrontational styles being used. Once people adopt set positions on points of principle or on arguments such meetings lose their usefulness. Using seating arrangements known to encourage this early polarisation of views is foolhardy in the extreme.

Clubs and societies

Meetings of organisations like these often depart quite widely from the normal rules of procedure and create difficulties for themselves in the process. If they are to function successfully, they should give some thought to the purpose of the meeting. There should be an agenda and the chairman should try to keep the meeting to it. Meetings may vary in size according to how many people are interested in turning up, and this inevitably makes the chairman's job more difficult. The location, too, may not be desirable from the point of view of having an effective meeting, as clubs and societies often have to meet in school classrooms or church halls or other places which have not been designed for meetings. They should put a time limit on the meeting, for in cases like this people tend to talk more – because of their enthusiasm for the activity the club or society has been formed to promote. Proceedings should pay a little more attention to things like rules of debate, motions, the quorum and reaching decisions than they commonly tend to. But a balance has to be struck: the last thing that is wanted is to deaden the keenness to meet in the first place, by imposing too strict a regime of rules.

The fullest possible participation should be encouraged, particularly of junior and new members, for they are the ones who will keep the club alive in the future. The chairman should try to strike a tactful balance between making progress by using a few rules and allowing people to express their thoughts and feelings about the club's affairs. The secretary should be as businesslike as it is possible for a part-time amateur to be without becoming too officious. Concise, clear minutes will help the club to know what it is doing and where it has come from. They will also be useful in the future when someone comes to write the history of the organisation.

Political and trade union meetings

Political parties and trade unions seem to be the worst offenders when it comes to having too many rules and following them too rigidly. I have even known a trades council meeting to start on Matters Arising from the Minutes at 7.30pm and still be discussing them at 10pm. Such meetings are self-evidently inefficient, and their purpose should be re-appraised. There is also a tendency to have monthly or other regular meetings whether there is business to discuss or not. Some provision for the cancellation of a meeting if there is insufficient business is desirable, but may be virtually impossible to obtain as members may see it as an attempt to deprive them of their democratic rights.

The chairman should work as briskly as he can through the agenda, whilst at the same time allowing an opportunity for members to chip in on an item when they want to. It does not help to give the impression that one is trying to steamroller things through without proper discussion. This calls for particular sensitivity on the part of the chairman in judging the right moment to call for a vote or for a decision. Often, if there is no one waiting to speak against a motion, he will be able to put it to the vote without much trouble. There is after all little point in continuing trying to persuade people when they have already made up their minds. And if no one wants to speak against, that is usually a sign that everybody is in favour of the proposition.

One problem can be a lengthy agenda for some meetings. Some consideration then needs to be given to deleting items which do not really need to be discussed. It may also be the case that more frequent meetings will help. This is one case where more meetings may, in fact, help to solve a problem.

In some cases, there is a regular agenda each time, which follows this kind of pattern:

1   Apologies
2   Minutes
3   Matters Arising
4   Correspondence
5   Secretary's Report
6   Treasurer's Report
7   Other Reports
8   Speaker
9   Any Other Business.

In such a situation, there is a case for placing the speaker as the last item on the agenda and having, in fact, two meetings – a business meeting and a meeting with a visiting speaker. It is inconvenient, as well as tempting fate by encouraging people to raise all kinds of items, to return to business once the meeting has moved away to talk about what is perhaps a quite different topic.

Conferences and seminars

These may range in attendance from a few dozen to a few hundred people. The pattern will be formal, with a set programme to follow, and perhaps even with time limits for the discussion of topics in order to ensure that the meeting does not spend all its time on a very few items. The event may split into smaller groups or syndicates for part of the time and then come back together for a plenary session.

Depending upon the type of conference, there can be a great deal of lobbying to secure support for particular motions. There will often be great use of procedural motions, and it is by no means uncommon for a conference chaired by a weak chairman to become bogged down in procedural wrangles and achieve very little as a consequence. Participants may experience difficulty in getting to speak if they are unable to 'catch the chairman's eye'. Often, after a conference has finished, a verbatim account of the proceedings will be produced and circulated to those who were present so that they may have a record of what happened.

Other meetings

In addition to the kinds of meetings discussed here, there are many others, many of which might not at first thought appear to be meetings. But it is the *purpose* of coming together which really decides whether a gathering is a meeting or not. As we have already seen, meetings take place when people have decisions to make, problems to solve, cases to put, and so on. So a meeting can take place over breakfast, or between two people in a taxi travelling from one place to another, over a drink, on the golf course, at trade exhibitions. In other words, a meeting can take place just about anywhere people can talk together.

Most of these meetings will require few procedural rules, but all will need to pay some attention to the basic requirements for a successful meeting. From what has been said so far, we can see that the main requirements are:

1 The purpose of the meeting must be clear to all present.
2 There should be an agenda which everyone knows, even if it is not written down.
3 The numbers attending should be kept to the minimum which everyone will accept.
4 The location should be of the right size – not too large and not too cramped.
5 The time a meeting will last should be broadly agreed by the participants in advance.

6   Everybody who attends should be properly briefed.
7   Apologies for absence should always be sent as a courtesy.
8   Lobbying for support should be done discreetly, as some people get offended if people canvass support too obviously.
9   The meeting should work through the agenda systematically and in a reasonably businesslike manner.
10 The minimum number of rules necessary for 9 to happen should be provided for.
11 Everybody present should, as far as is reasonable, be encouraged to participate in the meeting.
12 Action should result from a meeting and someone should be responsible for seeing that it does.

One kind of meeting which may present some difficulties is the disciplinary meeting. Here, formality is almost essential, unless it is a preliminary interview, in which case an informal but frank person-to-person discussion may obviate the need for a disciplinary interview anyway. The objective at this stage is, presumably, to lead to an improvement in personal performance. If this can be achieved without the unpleasantness of a formal disciplinary hearing, so much the better.

If a formal hearing is necessary, the proceedings will have to be conducted scrupulously according to the organisation's rules or there may be grounds for a successful appeal against the decision. Often a person has the right to be accompanied by 'a friend'. This 'friend' will almost certainly turn out to have legal qualifications.

11

Problems with Meetings

We considered in Chapter 1 the general dissatisfaction that many people feel about meetings. Clearly, this general dissatisfaction indicates the existence of certain problems with meetings. Some would say that there are almost as many problems as there are meetings. That might be a slight exaggeration, but certainly it is possible to identify a number of problems which crop up with depressing regularity.

We shall now consider these problems, see how they each arise and in which kinds of meetings, and then suggest a solution which should prevent the problem from arising again. In looking for solutions, it should be borne in mind that, very often, avoidance is better than cure. For instance, if the problem is identified as being caused by having the wrong person in the chair, it can be avoided by putting somebody else in the chair who has better chairmanship skills. In fact, we shall begin our survey of the problems by looking at the various ways in which the chairman can make life difficult for everyone else.

Becoming entangled in procedure

This happens in formal meetings which have perhaps *too many rules and procedures* rather than too few. It is common in national conferences, is nearly always the fault of the chairman for failing to keep the troops in order and insist that they follow proper procedure, and can lead to a meeting breaking down entirely.

The real solution is to prevent this in the first place by having a skilled chairman. If the problem has already arisen, however, it may be best to declare a short adjournment while the difficulties are sorted out and then to resume the meeting. It may also help in the longer term if the standing orders for the meeting can be reviewed, to see where they may be simplified.

Too many amendments

This is almost the same as becoming entangled in procedure, except that that can happen with rules generally and this concerns one particular form of confusion. When a chairman allows a meeting to discuss more than one amendment at once, he is asking for trouble. Again, it is common in large, formal meetings and is best avoided by having a different chairman.

Failing this, a short adjournment may be necessary while things are sorted out and the meeting can proceed. At the very least, the chairman has to establish a *priority order* for the amendments and make sure that the meeting sticks to this and that the discussion does not wander. It is best to discuss only one amendment but, if necessary, to allow participants to register with the chair a *notice of further amendment* which can be taken when the present amendment is disposed of.

Too many points of order

This is another problem which arises with large formal meetings, especially when there is a more than usually high degree of controversy in the proceedings and where a lot of people want to speak but cannot catch the chairman's eye. Raising a point of order and then trying to extend it into a short speech is a technique that desperate speakers will try with a weak chairman. It is common in political conferences.

One answer is a better chairman. Another is for the chairman to be reminded tactfully, perhaps by the secretary, that points of order must be restricted to disputes over the procedure of the meeting and must not be extended to its content. Since a chairman cannot refuse points of order, some way has to be found to remind him of the need to restrict their use to their proper purpose.

Confusion over what has been decided

This can happen in any meeting where there is controversy and attempts are made to find a formula of words for a motion which will command a support as wide as possible. Where similar motions on a subject at a conference are *composited*, or combined together into a single motion, it can also happen. Even in small meetings, it can occur if the discussion has ranged widely and the chairman has made little or no attempt to summarise the discussion before taking the sense of the meeting.

A good chairman will take pains to ensure that the meeting is crystal clear about what it has decided. Insisting that motions are written down can also help. It is even possible for a member of the meeting to help by asking a question like 'If we agree to this, Mr Chairman, does it mean that we are saying . . . ?' Keeping speeches short helps, as do simplified procedure, a clear sequence of amendments and a strict control over points of order.

Disruptive behaviour
This can be caused by intruders or infiltrators in a public meeting, but is more usually initiated by members of the meeting. A good chairman will spot the signs, because it rarely occurs without some kind of provocation, and will take early action either to defuse the situation or to deflect the disruption into a less destructive kind of activity. A proposal to defer consideration of the matter or to have a special enquiry into the facts may help.

If diversionary tactics do not help, a chairman may simply have to invoke his powers to control the meeting. A short adjournment may help people to cool off and give the chairman a chance to reassert his authority. In the last resort, the persons causing the disruption may have to be asked to leave. If they refuse to go and instead continue the disruption, stewards may have to eject them from a public meeting or the police may have to be called. In a private meeting, it would be highly unusual for this to have to be done. Adjournment is usually enough. It is, after all, difficult to continue disrupting a meeting that has broken up and therefore, for the time being at least, does not exist.

Uncertain openings and closings
Confusion about how to open a meeting often stems from slackness over the starting time. Even a weak chairman can help himself by following some easy steps:

1 At the time the meeting is scheduled to start (or as soon

thereafter as is practicable), the chairman checks that a quorum is present. If it is:

2   The chairman declares the meeting open, calls it to order and asks if there are any apologies for absence.

3   He reads the agenda, unless it has been circulated previously.

4   The secretary reads the minutes of the previous meeting, unless these have also been circulated.

5   The chairman then asks if the minutes can be taken as a true record. If not, corrections are taken. If so, he asks for any matters arising. When these have been dealt with:

6   The chairman introduces the first item on the agenda paper.

Closing a meeting is a little more difficult, for the chairman has to judge when all the business has been completed. Where there is 'Any Other Business' on the agenda, this can drag on a little. A chairman can help himself by asking people who raise points which require detailed consideration to place them as agenda items to the next meeting. When there are no more minor matters to discuss which cannot be deferred, the chairman declares the meeting closed. Before he does, he may remind those present of the date and time of the next meeting. He may also tell the secretary the time at which the meeting finished, for recording in the minutes.

Decisions are avoided
Almost any kind of meeting may be accused of trying to avoid coming to decisions. They may be reluctant for many reasons. The problem may be too intractable and complex to permit of easy solution. There may be political reasons for avoiding a decision, perhaps because there may be a strong adverse public reaction to it. Or it may be difficult to select a course of action because there are several attractive and competing possibilities.

If the chairman is neither willing nor able to bring the meeting to a decision, someone else may have to do it. The secretary is the first obvious choice because he sits next to the chairman and thus has, or should have, his ear. Failing this, any strong member of a meeting, provided he has the support of at least some of the others, can propose a clearly worded motion and insist on a vote. In a small meeting which does not habitually take votes, such as many daily business and management meetings, it may not even be necessary to do this: one can simply point out tactfully to the others present that time is being wasted and that, since time is money, they really ought to make progress and arrive at a decision.

Meetings are badly run

Sometimes meetings do not follow their own rules. The situation may stem from a genuine and sincere attempt to find short cuts, to avoid procedural wrangles and get clear-cut decisions. But, if continued, it can lead to a total breakdown of law and order within a meeting. If the rules cannot be followed, they should be changed. If they can be followed but people are reluctant to do this, for whatever reason, it is up to the chairman to lead them back to the straight and narrow path of observance of correct and jargon-free procedure.

If the chairman is not able to do this, the members of a meeting can help by reminding transgressors of the potential consequences of their action. Group pressures can be very powerful in persuading people to conform. If enough of the members of a meeting want to do things properly, that will go a long way towards securing an improvement in performance.

Meetings start late

In local authorities and other organisations where meetings are an important and integral part of their activities, meetings usually begin promptly. But in many others it may be as much as fifteen to thirty minutes after the appointed time that things really get going. Such delays may not matter much in voluntary clubs and societies, but where they occur in commercial and industrial organisations the costs of having people hanging around unnecessarily can, over a period of time, mount up alarmingly.

The remedy is for the secretary to remind the chairman when the time to start the meeting has arrived and for the chairman to begin the proceedings, provided there is a quorum present. It will also help if other members of the organisation can be persuaded of the importance of starting meetings promptly. Much may be gained in this direction if meetings are only held when necessary and if they are accordingly given a higher priority.

Meetings wander from the point

Once again, where this happens, it is usually the chairman's fault.

But if people try to introduce too many extraneous points, it may be difficult for him to keep them to the point. An unwritten agenda, too many similar agenda items and lack of clear rules for meetings procedure can all serve to complicate matters and make smooth progress more difficult to achieve.

If a better chairman is not available, the secretary can tactfully prompt the chairman into action. In more formal meetings, any member can try to get things back on course by raising an appropriate point of order challenging any irrelevance. It is also worth stressing that circulated, written agendas, the grouping of similar items under the same heading and clear rules help to prevent this problem arising.

Hidden objectives

The agenda indicates, either explicitly or by implication, what the objectives of a meeting are. In addition to these, as we have seen, individual members or groups of members will have other objectives which they wish to achieve, but which they will not reveal openly to the other people present. Examples might be that a member wishes to impress the others present with his ability in committee in order that they should nominate him for some office or position that is becoming vacant, or a group may wish to use a particular item in order to embarrass another group present. This latter hidden objective is common in meetings where there are rival political groupings.

The best way to deal with hidden objectives is to bring them out into the open for all to see. In this way, individuals or groups may back away and let the meeting make its decisions without undue influence from these other usually non-productive factors. Even if they do not, at least everyone will be able to see how any particular decision has been arrived at.

Lack of opportunity to participate

The more people there are attending a meeting, the less chance there is for each person to participate in the proceedings. Sometimes, even in smaller meetings, one or two individuals will dominate and take up most of the available speaking time. This is very frustrating for those who would like to take part but who do not have the confidence or the pushiness to break in.

The chairman should make it possible for everyone who wants to participate to have the opportunity. If he does not, then individuals can follow the advice given in Chapter 5 on how to participate in a meeting. Other members can help the situation, perhaps by tactfully pointing out to those who are hogging the floor that there are others who might like to get a word in. Often, people do not realise they are having too much to say until it is pointed out to them, such is their enthusiasm for their own point of view.

Conflict is encouraged

Some devious chairmen actively encourage conflict within a meeting because while the members are fighting amongst themselves it deflects attention from what the chairman is doing. What the chairman is doing is usually making the decisions himself, because the meetings spend all their time arguing and do not reach the decisions which have to be made. It means that the chairman gets his own way on most of the issues. Sometimes, however, conflict may be encouraged in a meeting for a rather more honourable purpose. In some cases, it can help an organisation if people can meet together and get things off their chests. This means that they may say harsh things to each other, but, in the hands of a sensitive and capable chairman, the outcome may be that people make a new start in their relationships with each other, see others' points of view more clearly and that morale is raised.

Where a chairman is simply being devious or vindictive, the best solution is to point this out in as tactful a manner as possible. However, where the chairman is the boss at work or someone else with the power to make others' lives less pleasant, it may be better to lobby the other members of the meeting discreetly in advance and try to ensure that conflict in the meetings is reduced to the point at which decisions can be made. In other words, the best way to deal with a devious chairman is to fight fire with fire and to become a little devious oneself.

Consensus and compromise reduce morale

In some organisations there can be a tendency to avoid conflict and dissent to such an extent that decisions are only made when those involved have reached a consensus or compromise view. This has advantages in that decisions have general support because everybody has had a say in making them. However, a common problem with this approach is that decisions tend to be cautious and conservative in their effects, and this can be very frustrating for those who want to see issues tackled more dynamically. This leads to a lowering of morale.

What is really needed is a proper balance between consensus and compromise when they are appropriate and a little more risk-taking when this is appropriate. If it can be agreed that certain activities can be delegated to individual members or to small groups of members, this will help to inject an element of life into the situation. Consensus and compromise are best kept for topics where there is a real danger of disruptive and unproductive conflict rather than being used as a general method of doing things.

Weak chairmanship
We have already discussed a number of problems which result from weak or poor chairmanship. A weak chairman will always produce problems in meetings and is therefore best removed so that someone else with more authority and control can be placed in the chair. The penalties for not doing this will be continuing problems, frustration, inefficiency and a lowering of morale.

Where this cannot be done, either because the chairman is the boss or it would cause unnecessary upset for other reasons (someone who has been chairman for many years may be offended by being removed, or members may wish to avoid treating someone who has been a loyal servant in a way which is, in effect, telling them that their services are no longer required), the other methods discussed above for circumventing the difficulties can be tried. Clearly, something has to be done. If all else fails, there may simply be no alternative to removing the chairman by whatever means are possible.

Meetings last too long
There is always a tendency for meetings to last longer than necessary. Once people have assembled together for the purpose of discussing matters of common interest, it is inevitable that they will remain together for a period of time. If tea or coffee is served during the meeting, this will ensure that the meeting lasts at least until everyone has finished drinking it. If there is a lengthy agenda, each

item will require a minimum amount of discussion time before it can be disposed of. If people are seated too comfortably, they may be reluctant to end the meeting and get back to other duties or activities.

One suggestion that has been made for curtailing the length of meetings is that they should be held standing up rather than sitting down. This may well work with meetings held during working hours, but it is difficult to see how it could apply to many other kinds of meetings. Perhaps one of the simplest and most effective methods is to agree upon an approximate (but realistic) finishing time before the meeting begins. During working hours, an effective device is to start the meeting one hour, say, before lunch.

The wrong people attend
In meetings at work it is often the case that people attend because of the positions that they hold. This can easily mean that because they have other commitments they send a deputy. Sometimes the deputy will be able to deal with all the topics that his superior could, but sometimes he will have a more limited role within his department and may not be able to deal with some of the topics which arise. It can also happen that, where people are elected to a committee, they are not necessarily the most able or most knowledgeable people available. Consequently, the proceedings of the meeting are impaired.

To try to ensure that the right people attend, it can help if the secretary checks in advance who will be attending. If he suspects that someone may not be able to help the meeting too much he can then have a word with the person who should really be present, to see if his other commitments can be varied to make it possible for him to attend. Where people attend because they have been elected, not much can be done to change their attendance. One of the drawbacks of democracy is that you have to accept what it produces.

There are too many meetings
This is a very common complaint in many kinds of organisations, particularly where a committee structure is used in decision-making. This can all too easily lead to the spawning of numbers of

sub-committees and working parties which add considerably to the number of meetings that people have to attend.

It is always worth asking 'Is this meeting really necessary?' Chairmen and secretaries have a special responsibility here to make sure that they are not inflicting meetings unnecessarily upon their members. It is also worth exploring some of the alternatives to meetings discussed in Chapter 14.

Meeting for the sake of meeting

This is a variation of the previous problem. Where a meeting has no other function than to rubber-stamp decisions that have been made elsewhere, it has little purpose. Unfortunately, it can be convenient to delegate many matters to committees or sub-committees and then to formalise those decisions at a meeting of the full organisation. Local authorities and university senates often operate in this way. It has the advantage that the primary body is relieved of a great deal of work, and it allows for a decision to be changed at the last minute if it is seen to be generating a lot of opposition or if further information emerges which means a decision is no longer appropriate.

Inability to reach a quorum

In many organisations it is laid down that a meeting cannot proceed if there is not a quorum of the members present. Where the minimum number of people necessary consistently fail to turn up, a serious problem is posed, for no decisions can be made. It is then up to the secretary to contact those who are not turning up and impress upon them the importance of attending. If this fails, an approach will have to be made to the next higher level of authority in the organisation, which may decide to disband a committee or sub-committee. If people are not prepared to attend, that is perhaps the best thing to do.

Poor preparation by members

If those who are to attend a meeting do not familiarise themselves with any papers circulated in advance, or if they do not otherwise prepare themselves for the meeting, this can lead to a situation in which a meeting is dominated too much by the one or two people who *have* prepared. It can also mean that the secretary or the chairman has to give an unnecessarily detailed briefing on each item. Involving all those present in the business of the meeting is perhaps the best way of ensuring that, if they turn up, they will have prepared properly, for this will be the only way in which they can avoid looking rather silly or inadequate. Few people will want to be shown up in public, which is the net effect of being brought into the discussions by the chairman.

Too much paperwork

There is a common problem with local government meetings and, indeed, in the meetings of any organisations which have a complex committee structure. There are minutes of previous meetings, minutes of sub-committees, reports on matters for decision, and various other items for the information of members. It soon piles up into a volume of printed material in which it may be difficult to separate the key items from the less important ones.

Much can be done by chairmen who insist on having a meeting with the secretary and other officers beforehand and refuse to put items on the agenda if there really is no need for them to be considered by the meeting. A chairman should also ensure that, when the papers are sent out, no officer is allowed to bring a report to the meeting and expect it to be considered when the members clearly have not had the chance to read it in advance. Only short and very urgent items should be allowed to be brought to a meeting for emergency consideration. Even then, major matters may be better dealt with by calling another, special meeting of the committee.

The high cost of meetings

Unless people are attending a meeting in a purely voluntary capacity in their own time, there is always a cost to meetings. This can be quite horrendous in organisations where highly paid individuals meet together regularly for long periods. It can be quite a salutary exercise to calculate how much a meeting costs!

The remedy is to re-organise affairs in such a way that fewer and shorter meetings are required. Failure to do so means that the organisation continues to work under an unnecessary burden. As Chapter 14 shows, there are alternatives to meetings which will meet the needs of many situations.

12

Analysing Meetings

If you are using this book as a course text, it will be appropriate at this point if the group attends a meeting in order to observe it and to analyse it in the way suggested in this chapter. If you are working through the book on your own it will be useful if you, too, can attend a meeting for the purpose of observing and analysing it. Groups may organise an outing to sit in on a local council committee meeting to which the public are admitted or they may like to hold a mock meeting of their own for videotaping and playback. Individuals may attend a meeting of the local council or they may simply apply the process of analysis to a meeting they would have to attend in the normal course of events.

The reason for doing this is that a great deal can be learned about how to improve an activity if the reasons for failure to be completely effective and the reasons for success can both be understood. To achieve this, you need two things. You need a method of analysis and you need a number of aspects of an activity to apply the method to.

The method of critical analysis suggested here comprises four steps and seeks the answers to the following kinds of questions:

1 *Content:* What matters did the meeting consider? What information did those attending the meeting have? Who was present? Where and when was the meeting held? What decisions were made?
2 *Intentions:* Why was the meeting held? What were its objectives? Were these objectives worthwhile? Were they stated explicitly or merely implied?

3 *Treatment:* How was the meeting conducted? Were members encouraged to participate? Were there strict rules of procedure? Could the chairman have acted differently at any point? How were roles assigned in the meeting (e.g. secretary, treasurer, minutes taker)?

4 *Evaluation:* How well did the meeting proceed? If it failed, how, where and why did it fail? What changes, if any, might have improved the content, intentions or method of conducting the meeting?

There may well be other questions that you wish to ask, but these will serve as a basis on which to begin the analysis. You should also find it useful to complete the rating scale in Figure 13. Those who are part of a group will be able to compare assessments. They may even produce a group average for the assessment by collecting all the individual assessments together and collating them. This will enable us to analyse the meeting as a whole, but it will also be useful to study a number of particular points.

Assessing preparation

Let us begin our analysis of these individual features by considering how well those attending the meeting had prepared for it. It will help in considering this and the various aspects which follow if we again pose a series of questions for which you should seek answers. It will further help if we do this under the four headings used above:

1 *Content:*
   What information had been given in advance to those attending?
   Did this information appear to be adequate?
   What kinds of preparation had those attending apparently done?
   What kinds of special research?
   Which of those attending appeared to lack any preparation?

2 *Intentions:*
   What objectives did those present appear to have in preparing/ not preparing?
   Had any members of the meeting misunderstood the objectives of the meeting in their preparation?

Fig. 13 Analysing meetings rating scale

Rate the following aspects of the conduct of a meeting on a scale of 1 to 10, giving the highest marks for the most effective performance. Place a X in the appropriate box.

	1	2	3	4	5	6	7	8	9	10
Clarity of purpose or objectives of meeting										
Appropriateness of agenda										
Appropriateness of size of meeting										
Appropriateness of attendance of meeting										
Appropriateness of venue										
Appropriateness of length of meeting										
Quality of chairman										
Quality of minutes										
How well those present had prepared										
Pace of meeting (low score = too slow)										
Appropriateness of sequence of items										
Clarity of motions										
Adherence to rules										
Clarity of decisions										
Amount of participation by ordinary members										

	1	2	3	4	5	6	7	8	9	10
Quality of debate										
Ease of getting a word in edgeways										
Efficiency of secretary										
Clarity of action to be taken after meeting										
Quality of any reports and other papers prepared for the meeting										
Over-all assessment of the meeting										
Totals										

3 *Treatment:*

How had those present set about preparing for the meeting, so far as you could tell?

Had they prepared for all items on the agenda or only certain ones?

Were there any items for which no one had done any preparation?

What were the effects of this?

4 *Evaluation:*

How well had those present prepared for the meeting?

How could they have been better prepared?

Had anyone over-prepared?

Did the chairman and secretary appear to have had a pre-meeting briefing session?

Achievement of objectives

Let us look now at the objectives of the meeting and at how far these were achieved:

1 *Content:*

What were the objectives of the meeting?

Were these stated explicitly or were they implied?

Were they reasonable objectives for the meeting to expect to achieve?

Did everyone present appear to understand the objectives?

2   *Intentions:*

Did there appear to be a reason for the objectives being explicit/ implicit?

Was there any evidence of anyone present having hidden objectives?

What were these hidden objectives?

3   *Treatment:*

Did the meeting pay any conscious regard to its objectives?

Did anyone seek to divert the meeting from its objectives?

Who contributed most to the achievement of the objectives of the meeting?

4   *Evaluation:*

To what extent did the meeting achieve its objectives?

What could have been done to enable the meeting to achieve its objectives more fully?

What could have been done to neutralise any hidden objectives which were present?

Sequence of items

The success or failure of a meeting can hinge on the order in which it does its business, so it is worth applying the process of analysis to the sequence of items:

1   *Contents:*

What was the sequence of agenda items?

Which were the important items? Where were they placed?

Were there any emergency/confidential items?

Where were they placed?

2   *Intentions:*

Why were items in the order they were?

Were any items placed in such a position as to divert attention from them? Why do you think this was?

3   *Treatment:*

Did the chairman keep to the stated sequence of items? If he departed from it, why was this?

Did anyone seek to abuse 'Any Other Business' if this was an item on the agenda?

Were any items withdrawn? If so, why was this? Do you think the reason given was the real reason?

4 *Evaluation:*

Were items in the best order possible?

Could the order have been changed with benefit?

What would have been the best way to do this?

Dealing with agenda items

How each item is dealt with is an important consideration in analysing a meeting. It is an area in which there are many possible courses of action:

1 *Content:*

What was the content of each agenda item?

Was there sufficient information available on each item?

Was each item dealt with separately or were any items taken together? If they were taken together, why was this?

Did the chairman control the pace of the meeting?

2 *Intentions:*

Was it clear why each item was on the agenda?

Did the chairman try to steamroller any items through?

Did any people present appear to have made up their minds in advance on any items?

3 *Treatment:*

Was the appropriate amount of attention given to each item?

Did any items receive too much or too little attention?

If there was no 'Any Other Business' on the agenda, why do you think this was?

Were all the minor items treated in the same way?

4 *Evaluation:*

Could the chairman have acted differently on any item? What could he have done?

Was the content of each item appropriate or should any have been supported by more information?

Was the pace of the meeting appropriate to the amount of business to be done and the wish of those present to participate in the proceedings?

Clarity of decisions

No matter how well run a meeting is in terms of following its own procedures, it will have largely failed if it is not exactly clear what has been decided:

1   *Content:*
    What decisions were made?
    Were the decisions recorded by someone at the time?
    Were any items passed over without decision?
2   *Intentions:*
    Was everyone seeking to arrive at clear decisions?
    Was anyone seeking to fudge an issue?
3   *Treatment:*
    How were decisions made? By show of hands? By ballot? By the chairman taking the sense of the meeting?
    Did the chairman assume at any time that silence on the part of those present implied agreement with what was being proposed?
4   *Evaluation:*
    How clearly were decisions made?
    Could anything have been done to improve the clarity of the decisions?
    Could the method of making decisions have been improved?

Length of meeting

It is difficult to say how long a meeting should be in terms of hours and minutes, but if the length is appropriate for a proper discussion of all the items, then that is probably the best kind of guide:

1   *Content:*
    How long did the meeting last?
    How much time was spent on each item?
    Which items had the most/least time spent on them?
    Did the time spent on each item permit a proper discussion of the item?
    Were any items rushed through?
2   *Intentions:*
    Was anyone trying to filibuster/guillotine any item?

Was anyone trying to lengthen or shorten the meeting unduly?

3 *Treatment:*

How did the chairman apportion the time for each item?

What effect did other people present have on the amount of time spent on each item?

4 *Evaluation:*

Could the meeting have been shortened without loss?

Should more time have been spent on any item?

Was there a tendency for items involving large sums of money to go through on the nod whilst items involving quite small sums were debated at length?

Participation

If meetings are to continue to play a useful part in an organisation's affairs, they need to give each person present a chance to participate in the proceedings:

1 *Content:*

Using the Contribution Rate Chart in Figure 14, calculate who are the high contributors.

What differences are there in terms of age or seniority?

What differences are there between men and women?

What other differences can be noted in the contributions?

2 *Intentions:*

Do any members appear to have attended with the set purpose of contributing a lot or a little?

Do any appear to have attended with the set purpose of saying nothing at all?

Did the chairman appear to want everyone to participate?

3 *Treatment:*

What techniques were used by those who were high contributors when they wished to speak?

What techniques were used by low contributors when they wished to speak?

What techniques did the chairman use with someone he did not want to speak?

If the chairman was one who tries to involve everyone in the meeting, what techniques did he use to achieve this?

Fig. 14 Contribution rate chart

	Tally of contributions	**Total**
Example	ɪɪɪɪ ɪɪɪɪ 111	13
Chairman		
Vice-Chairman		
Secretary		
Treasurer		
Other officers (*specify*):		
1		
2		
3		
4		
5		
6		
Members (*name*):		
1		
2		
3		
4		
5		
6		
7		
8		
9		
10		
11		
12		
13		
14		
15		
16		
(*add to list as required for larger meetings*)	**Total**:	

4   *Evaluation:*

How successful was the chairman in sharing out the floor time amongst those present?

What could he have done to be more successful?

What could be the uses of a Contribution Rate Chart to a chairman? To other participants in a meeting?

Action after the meeting

It may be difficult to do this if you have observed a meeting of an organisation with whose procedures you are not familiar, but it will still be useful to attempt some analysis of what was likely to happen after the meeting:

1   *Content:*

What procedures did there appear to be for seeing that the meeting's decisions were carried out after the meeting had finished?

Did the secretary appear to be using any kind of action sheet?

Did any of those present at the meeting offer to be responsible for seeing that certain things were done?

Did you notice any gaps in the provision for seeing that action followed a decision?

Was there any evidence that actions decided at previous meetings had not, in fact, been carried out?

What explanations or excuses were offered for any such inactivity?

2   *Intentions:*

Did the meeting appear to be talk-oriented or action-oriented (that is, was the meeting simply a talking shop or did it intend to get things done)?

Was the meeting seen as a one-off or as part of an ongoing process?

Was the purpose of any proposed actions clear to all those present?

3   *Treatment:*

Were the decisions of the meeting recorded in such a way that it was clear who had to do what after the meeting?

How much of the work was to be done by the secretary and how much by others present?

What were the causes of any confusions over who had to do what?

What effect did these confusions have on the meeting and who attempted to resolve them? The chairman or someone else who was present?

Fig. 15   Conclusions from attending a meeting

1   This meeting did not seem to have any clear purpose, much less a set of objectives to achieve. Things go better when everyone knows what they are wanting to do.

2   The agenda was far too long for the meeting to get through it in reasonable time. It is often better to meet more frequently if agendas are getting too long.

3   There were too many people at the meeting. If meetings are too big, it prevents everyone contributing fully.

4   The room was far too small. Rooms should be appropriate in size to the numbers expected to attend.

5   The meeting went on far too long. People lose interest in organisations where meetings are interminable.

6   The chairman had no idea how to chair a meeting. Where chairmen are elected, people should choose someone with the requisite skills.

7   The minutes of the previous meeting were far too long and incoherent. Minutes should be as concise as possible and concentrate on recording decisions.

8   Too many of the people there did not appear to have read the papers which were circulated before the meeting. Meetings cannot be effective if those present do not prepare properly for them.

9   The pace of the meeting was far too slow. There is no need to rush through items, but a reasonable pace should be maintained.

10   The agenda was upside down. Trivial items were at the beginning of the meeting and some vital items were left until last, when half the members had gone.

11   There was no attempt by the chairman to make sure that the resolutions were accurately recorded by the secretary.

12   The rules of debate were not followed. People were, for instance, allowed to make lengthy speeches in the guise of points of order.

13   No one seemed to know what had been decided. Certainly, those observing had no idea what was going on.

14   Only half a dozen people present spoke. Half the others seemed either to be asleep or to be filling in their claims forms for attendance allowances and expenses.

15   Over-all the meeting was rambling, unstructured and tedious. A lesson in what not to do if ever I saw one.

4 *Evaluation:*

How well did the meeting provide for what had to be done after the meeting?

How could it have provided more effectively for subsequent action?

What different steps would you have taken to provide for effective action after the meeting if you had been the chairman or the secretary?

When you have completed your analysis of these and any other aspects of the meeting which you wish to consider, make an analysis of the meeting as a whole. Then make a list of all the things you have learned about meetings and committee procedure from this analysis. An example of a typical list of what might have been learned from observing a poorly conducted meeting is given in Figure 15.

13

Preparing and Presenting Reports to Meetings

Most of what happens in meetings centres around the use of the spoken word as people make proposals and counter proposals, amend them, argue about them and (usually) work towards the point at which a decision will be made. Much of this activity, however, would be impossible in most organisations if there were not reports on the various topics up for discussion. Reports are an integral part of the meetings process. If the information and argument they contain were not available it would become impossible to make a decision at all on many occasions. So it is important that reports should be clearly and competently written. If you have meetings to attend, you will almost certainly – if not now, at some point in the future – have reports to write. For this reason, this chapter offers guidance in the techniques of writing effective reports.

Reports, once written, need to be presented to those who will have to make decisions on their contents. Even where reports are circulated in advance, the report writer will usually be given the opportunity at a meeting to present his report and draw out and highlight the points he feels are particularly important. So this chapter also offers guidance in the techniques of presenting reports effectively.

Techniques of effective writing

It is clearly beyond the scope of this book to provide training in the techniques of writing. For this you will need to consult one of the books on writing listed in the Further Reading section. It is possible, however, to outline some of the main techniques that will increase the chances that whatever you write will be accurate, clear, concise and, therefore, effective.

Essentially, you need to do ten things if you are to improve the quality and effectiveness of your writing:

1   You need to keep the reader firmly in mind as you write and write for him.
2   You need a strategy for writing that enables you to approach the task of writing a report (or anything else for that matter) systematically and in a manner that makes efficient use of your time.
3   You should use a pattern of organisation which suits your purposes in writing (we shall look at the planning of a report shortly).
4   You should construct your paragraphs so that, most of the time, the key (or topic) sentence comes at the beginning, where it receives natural emphasis simply by being at the beginning (though it is important to change the structure and length of paragraphs for the sake of variety).
5   You should construct sentences so that the average length is less than twenty words (though here again variety in length and structure is important).
6   You should choose short words in preference to longer ones (whenever you have a choice).
7   You should write with due regard for what is grammatically appropriate (it is a little old-fashioned to talk about 'correctness' in grammar as so many aspects have become the subject of controversy).
8   You should use punctuation so that it helps in conveying your meaning to your readers. This usually means that you need to keep it as simple as possible – do not worry if you are not really sure when to use colons and semi-colons, you can achieve a great deal simply with commas and full stops.
9   You should spell correctly. Some people don't worry about this because they think the typist will correct any errors, but you cannot rely on this happening and readers may infer that an inability to spell correctly is symptomatic of other, more serious failings.

10 When you have written something, check and check again for errors and deficiencies until there is no more time and it simply has to leave you to begin its journey to its readers.

A strategy for report writing

In addition to following the advice listed above, you will write more effective reports for meetings if you follow a five-step strategy. The strategy has the mnemonic title PAPER and is described in full detail in *Report Writing* by Gordon Wainwright (Management Update, 1984), but, briefly, it comprises the following steps:

1 **Prepare**   Define terms of reference for the report, obtain a clear picture of who will read the report, set objectives for the report to achieve, collect and store all the information that you need.
2 **Assess**   Before you proceed to the next step, try to find time to pause and let what you have done mull over in your mind – twenty-four hours is usually about right (this is known as an incubation period and helps you in evaluating what you have done – you can usefully insert an assessment stage or incubation period between each of the remaining stages of this strategy).
3 **Plan**   From all the information you have collected, select that which you need for your report, organise it logically, giving a heading for each section that will ultimately comprise the body of the report, and make provision for the following sections in the order given:
   Summary, giving all essential points;
   Introduction, giving purpose, scope and plan of treatment of report;
   Body of report, giving the facts discovered, grouped under appropriate headings (*never* use the term 'Body of Report' as a heading in the report itself);
   Conclusion, giving conclusions formed on the basis of the facts and any recommendations.
   (More complex reports will inevitably need more complex structures, but this simple plan will suit most reports.)
4 **Express**   Write the report in as short a time as possible (so that you can be sure of retaining throughout the same concept of

what you are trying to say); write the parts of the report in the following order:

Body of Report
Introduction
Conclusion
Summary

Follow the advice already given on the techniques of effective writing: keep the report as short as it can be without missing out anything that is relevant, use appropriate illustrative material to enliven the report and, once again, keep the needs of your readers in mind at all times.

5 **Review** Carry out a detailed check of the report in terms of how it is structured or organised and see that the technicalities of expression (grammar, punctuation and spelling) are followed. Check that every statement in the report means what it is supposed to mean, assess the readability of the report (make sure that the average sentence length is less than twenty words and that the number of long words has been kept to the absolutely necessary minimum), and re-write any parts of the report which require it. Decide upon the layout and method of reproducing the report, and submit the report in good time for it to be sent out with the other papers for the meeting.

Followed carefully, this strategy should result in reports which are, as we said at the beginning and emphasise again now, accurate, clear, concise and effective. Somehow, taking the requisite degree of care seems to be easier when it is done within the context of a systematic approach.

Once they are written and typed or printed in their final version, reports can then be circulated, ready to be presented to the meeting. It is to this vital step that we now turn.

Presenting reports to meetings

What is now required is in a sense another version of the report, because, even if those attending the meeting have not actually read the report (and some may not have), it will not be appropriate to follow the written structure when presenting it orally. What is needed is a structure which is simpler and which still covers all the important points.

In an oral report, for that is what we are now dealing with, a three-part structure is common. This consists of:

1 *Introduction*
2 *Body of Report*
3 *Conclusion*

This pattern follows the standard advice given to public speakers, whatever their subject or the setting in which they are speaking:

> Tell them what you are going to tell them (i.e. introduction), tell them (i.e. body of report or speech), and then tell them what you've told them (i.e. conclusion).

Audio-visual aids, as appropriate, should be used at the points where they make the greatest impact.

There are differences in the ways in which written and oral reports are expressed. Slang and colloquialisms are totally inappropriate in written reports, but this may not necessarily be the case in oral reports. The style of speaking has to be much more direct and the report presenter needs to judge from the audience he has in front of him, in a way that a writer cannot, just how best to make his points. You will need to talk to your listeners in the way that you and they will find the most natural, and the one that will best establish a favourable rapport between you. If you do not do this and try to speak too formally, you may well find that you lose the attention of your listeners. This will be bound to limit how effectively you can express yourself.

One thing you must *never* do is simply read your report out aloud. Few audiences, even those who have not bothered to read the report, will be prepared to tolerate this. What you should do instead is to make notes on what you want to say and speak from these. By all means, if you find it helpful, use the same headings you have used in the body of the written report or a highlighter to draw your attention to the points you wish to stress, but use these as a guide only. After all, the purpose of the notes is simply to guard against your forgetting exactly what it was you wanted to say. It is not to provide you with a rigid framework, though certain key words and telling phrases are worth underlining or highlighting with a coloured pen.

Do not try to memorise what you want to say, for this will make you sound stilted and artificial. Having said this, it is often worthwhile memorising your introduction because, if you are at all nervous (and nearly everyone is when speaking in public), this will at least get you started into your presentation. Once you are up and running, as it were, it is much less likely that you will falter and dry up. Your notes will help to prevent this in any case. If you have any fears of drying up while you are speaking, rehearse your presentation at least once beforehand. Do it in front of a mirror so that you can gain some idea of how it might look to others. Tape it if you can. In this way, you will also be able to play it back and hear how it sounds. Best of all, videotape your presentation. If you can then play this back to yourself, in the presence of a sympathetic but critical friend, you should learn a great deal about how you will appear and sound to your audience. There are many lessons to be learned by a speaker from a videotape of himself. You should also find that doing this sort of thing increases your confidence in being able to perform well in the actual meeting.

There are several other fairly standard hints and tips on effective speaking in public settings which may be of use to you:

1 Number the sheets of your notes and either have them typed in a large-size typeface or write them out so that they will be legible when you are standing up and they are on the table in front of you.
2 Speak clearly, but not loudly, so that everyone in the room can hear you. Watch for signs that people furthest away are having difficulty in hearing you.
3 Nerves sometimes make your mouth feel dry before you begin and, if there is no glass of water handy, relax your lower jaw for a few moments. This will cause your mouth to water, usually, and if it does the dryness will go away. You may even be able to suck a sweet before it will be your turn to speak.
4 You should not be too worried if you pause at any point to find out precisely where you have got to in your notes. Pauses invariably sound longer to speakers than they do to listeners and, in any event, a pause can be a very effective device for letting what you have said sink home. Remember not to speak too quickly and pay particular attention to selecting short, simple words to put your message over.
5 If you are using any statistics, remember that audiences have great difficulty in absorbing this kind of information. Keep

them to an absolute minimum. Best not to use them at all if you can avoid it, but if you cannot, consider the advantages of putting them on an overhead projector transparency or a wall chart. Essential statistical data should, of course, be included in your written report.

6   Take care over your body language. Look at the audience as much as you can and not at the wall at the back of the room. Keep your facial expressions lively. Use open gestures and postures. Keep your back reasonably straight. Dress smartly, but don't overdress. Try to eliminate 'ums', 'ers' and 'ahs' from your speech. Don't wander about too much, but don't feel that you have to remain rooted to the spot. Try not to rustle your notes too much or fiddle with other objects like pens, pockets or even your own chin.

7   Your audience are human beings like yourself and if you treat them as such and talk *to* them rather than at them they will tend to reward you with their attention and ultimate approval.

8   If they ask you questions afterwards, answer them clearly and directly and concisely. No one wants another speech as an answer to a question.

9   Remember that accuracy, clarity, conciseness and simplicity are even more important in oral reports than they are in written reports.

10 Concentrate on evidence and rational argument rather than appeals to emotion or prejudice. This is much more likely to sway an audience than any kind of silver-tongued oratory.

These hints may help, but if you know what you are talking about, prepare your material carefully and speak with notes you will avoid most of the potential pitfalls that await the unwary. If, in addition, you can rehearse what you are going to say and anticipate any questions, this should overcome any remaining problems. You are giving a performance, so rehearsal is a necessary and appropriate element in the activity. If you follow this advice, the meetings you are reporting to will be more efficiently and effectively conducted and will thus contribute to the over-all success and effectiveness of the organisation, whether this is a small club or society or a large local authority or a business organisation of whatever form. Any organisation can benefit from reports which are better written and better presented.

14

Alternatives to Meetings

It may seem strange that in a book on meetings and committee procedure one should consider *not* holding meetings at all, but there are alternatives. Because meetings are such expensive and time-consuming events it is always worth any organisation's while to explore the possibilities of avoiding them, especially if this can lead to a more efficient and effective use of time.

There are at least fourteen alternatives to meetings and there are two other things which can be done to make the meetings that have to be attended more useful. In this chapter, we shall explore these alternatives and the methods of improving meetings when no alternative exists. We shall look at the advantages and disadvantages of each alternative, and the circumstances under which each is most and also least useful. In this way, you should be able to eliminate, or at least help to eliminate, unnecessary meetings in your own organisation.

Whether a meeting takes place or not, one question has to be answered satisfactorily: *Is your meeting really necessary?* This chapter will help you to answer that question.

Delegating

Certain activities can often be delegated to other individuals who report back to their boss or to a committee at intervals rather than continuously. Decisions taken by individuals in this way can remove much of the need for group action. The terms of reference within which the authority to decide and act is delegated need to be

specified, together with the limits upon that delegation. For instance, a committee may delegate the authority to one of its officers to
spend money in certain ways, but it will usually place an upper limit
on the amount that can be spent before the matter has to be brought
before the committee for decision.

The advantages of delegation are that it speeds up decision-
making and therefore action, it reduces the frequency of meetings,
it gives people more responsibility which increases job satisfaction,
and it enables committees to concentrate on policy formulation and
to avoid getting bogged down in the detail of the day-to-day running
of an organisation. The disadvantages are that decisions may be
taken too hastily on some occasions, committee members may
become dissatisfied because they meet so infrequently that they just
do not feel involved in the organisation any more, officers may
acquire too much power compared with that remaining with committee members, and members may come to have a poor picture of
how the organisation actually operates.

Delegation is most useful (indeed necessary) in large organisations in which it is impossible for one person or one group of people
to maintain control over all the organisation's activities. It is also
useful where speed of response and action is more desirable than a
slow, careful weighing of the pros and cons of what to do. It is least
useful where it is important for as many people as possible to be
involved in the decision-making. This may be the case in clubs and
societies where half the fun in being a member is that you get to
participate in all the decision-making.

Telephone calls

Sometimes, rather than call everyone together for a meeting, you
can telephone them and test their opinions on a decision that has to
be made. This can work where there is a single problem to be
resolved, question to be answered or issue to be considered. It
cannot work with long, complex agendas. It requires the person
making the calls to spend a large amount of time making the calls,
but since those being called spend a little time each on the call, the
total contact minutes will be less than it would if everyone met
together to consider the matter.

So the advantages of using the telephone are that it saves time, it focuses people's attention on a specific issue, and it involves everyone in the decision without their having to go to the inconvenience of meeting. Disadvantages are that, since no one but the person making the call knows exactly what everyone has said, misinterpretation (or deliberate deceit) could result in a decision being taken which does not in fact accurately reflect the views of the group; it can only be applied to one matter at a time unless confusion is to be risked; it ties up the telephone for incoming calls, which might be an important consideration in a small business; and it places too much responsibility upon the shoulders of one person.

Telephone calls are most useful where people live a long way apart or are disabled or do not have the same working hours. They are least useful where the matter to be discussed is complex, where there are several things to be decided, when you want to be sure that everyone understands the issue and agrees with the decision made, and when you want to share the responsibility for decision-making amongst everybody and make sure everybody realises it is a common responsibility.

Teleconferencing

This is an extension of the idea of telephoning people and is a facility which enables a number of people to speak to each other simultaneously on their telephones. It thus enables people to meet without actually leaving their offices.

Teleconferencing means time is not wasted in travelling to and from meetings, people living far apart (even in different countries) can 'meet' together easily, it is more likely that key individuals can talk together rather than having to use deputies because of the pressure of other appointments, and a range of matters can be covered easily and quickly. However, teleconferencing can be expensive to establish as a system and it can be expensive to run, so it is really only attractive when highly paid individuals need to talk together. It also loses the various values of face-to-face contact between people and makes things seem a little cold and remote, and if more than one person speaks at once it can be impossible to hear properly what is said.

It is most useful therefore, when those meeting are busy

executives whose time is at a premium. It is least useful where it is felt to be important that people should meet face-to-face and really get to know each other and understand each other's attitudes and points of view. Teleconferencing may become a more widely acceptable alternative to meetings if (or when?) video telephones become a viable and cheap proposition. One of the attractions of meetings is that you can see the people who are helping you to make decisions and this kind of facility will therefore make teleconferencing more attractive.

The 'nil return'

In some circumstances, instead of meeting when there is no need to, those who would otherwise meet together can submit a 'nil return' to indicate that they have no problems or no questions that they wish to raise for general consideration. In this way, meetings may be cancelled if there is not enough business for them to be useful. Agenda items can be carried forward to the next meeting, which can be held when a more reasonable amount of business has been accumulated. This can be done in organisations which have a systematic approach to delegation.

The advantages are that it saves having unnecessary meetings, it increases the pace of organisational activity because people can then attend to other aspects of their work, and it reduces the frustration many busy people experience from having to attend too many meetings. Disadvantages are that some people may be tempted to put in a 'nil return' to save having a meeting when they really ought to report something, people may become remote from each other and out of touch with each other's problems simply because they do not see each other as much as they ought to, and people may feel less involved in the organisation.

'Nil returns' are best for avoiding meetings on trivial routine matters when things are going all right and no problems are arising. It would clearly be an inefficient use of human resources to meet in such circumstances. They are of less value when the fact that people meet together means that they often find, just by talking, that they do, in fact, have a common problem and can then begin to identify a solution for it.

Computer access

Where meetings are held to exchange or to issue information or instructions, it may be possible for the information or instructions to be recorded in a central computer to which every individual has access from his own terminal. The information or instructions can be updated at regular intervals, perhaps every day, and those concerned can be told that they should access the material at a pre-determined time.

The advantages of this are that large amounts of information can be transferred quickly, especially if each work station has a printer; the material can be kept bang up to date; and people need only concern themselves with the information or instructions which relate to them. Disadvantages include the fact that this is a very cold and impersonal method of imparting information or instructions; people can become alienated; those giving instructions may tend to become a little too authoritarian in their attitudes and their methods, and may further alienate people; and the communication which takes place tends to be only one-way.

It is best used when people request the supply of large amounts of information very quickly or people are out of their offices a lot and some reliable method of leaving messages for them is needed. It is of least use where it is important that people should know each other well and should interact in a friendly and purposeful manner. Some of the disadvantages of this method of avoiding meetings may be overcome when computers become more interactive.

The one-man band

It is often said that the most efficient committee is a committee of one. It is not very democratic, but it is certainly true that one person on his or her own, with no need to consult others, can get through a great deal of business in a very short time.

The principal advantages where one person has over-all authority are that there is no need for time-wasting committees, there can be direction and decisiveness in the organisation's affairs, and conflicts between different departments in an organisation can be controlled. On the other hand, there is no involvement and participation by other members of the organisation, and this can generate frustrations and dissatisfaction; there will be a tendency for work not to be done when the person in charge is not present; and people will become increasingly reluctant to show initiative and take risks.

The one-man band is appropriate in activities like editing a newspaper or journal or in producing a play, where arguments about what to do could well mean that publication time or play time comes and everybody is still arguing. Somebody has to be given the authority to keep things moving. It is least appropriate and effective where people need to co-operate and consult and regard each other as equals.

Seeing people

Instead of calling a meeting, it may be possible to go and see people in their own offices or places of work. People will often be more forthcoming when interviewed individually on their own territory where they feel secure.

Going to see people shows them you care enough about what they have to say to put yourself to the trouble of going to ask them; it means you get information 'from the horse's mouth'; you see how what they say relates to the context within which they operate; and by seeing several people regularly you build up a broad, accurate and up-to-date picture of what is going on in the organisation. On the other hand, they see only their own concerns and problems, they may think that you regard what they do as being more important than other aspects of the organisation's work, they may think they have more influence with you than they actually do, and because they see you on their own territory they may have an advantage in any difference of opinion (people perform better in arguments on their own territory).

Seeing people is most appropriate if you are a new manager in an organisation and you want to know precisely how things work. It is least suitable where you have a heavy workload yourself and are highly paid. In that case, going to see people is much more expensive than calling them all together for regular conferences.

Newsletters

Newsletters work as an alternative to meetings where the meetings are mainly for the purpose of giving information or progress reports. They can be a less expensive method of keeping everyone in the picture.

They can be used to enhance the organisation's image with its members, and they can convey large amounts of information in relatively little space; they can also show people what is happening through the use of photographs and other static visual methods, and they can encourage feedback by encouraging people to write letters or articles. But they have to appear at regular intervals if they are to be useful (if people do not know when to expect them they will put them to the back of their minds), and they are limited in the two-way nature of the communication they can provide. People may also see them simply as a form of organisational propaganda and ignore them for that reason.

They are best for large organisations where people are spread over a wide geographical area and there are really too many of them to call them to a meeting to pass on the same information. They are least useful when the group is relatively small and meets frequently in the course of the day's work anyway.

Memos

Rather than call a meeting, it may be sufficient simply to send a memo to everyone concerned. This can be quick and convenient and they can read it at a time that best suits them, unless it is an urgent instruction or request, in which case they will clearly read and act on it straightaway.

Memos can, given reasonable internal communications, get information or instruction to people in less time than it might take to call a meeting, they provide a permanent record of what people were told and when they were told it, and mean that everybody is informed in precisely the same way. However, they are less personal and more distant than a meeting, they provide less opportunity for feedback to ensure that the recipients have understood the contents, and they may fail to communicate properly because, like reports, they are often badly written.

They are most useful where a small amount of information or instruction is to be given and where a record for future reference is needed. They are of least use if you want to motivate people and make them feel that they are genuinely involved in what is going on and that their opinions matter.

Videos

Because these are capable of carrying moving pictures as well as static displays, they can present information which newsletters and memos cannot. They can do it in a more interesting way as well.

People will be more prepared to watch a video than read either a newsletter or a memo. Nowadays videos are becoming quicker and cheaper to produce in-house, soundtracks in different languages can be recorded to accompany the same visual content, and people can also see those giving the information, if desired. But they are still a one-way channel, they can be expensive to produce if the information is detailed and if a professional standard of presentation is required, and since people have to set aside the time to watch them they may try to defer this and possibly forget to watch at all.

Videos are best for promotional or propaganda purposes. They are least useful for situations where understanding of the content needs to be tested in some way and where people need to be motivated and involved in activities. Some of the drawbacks to videos may be overcome when interactive television systems are more widely available.

'Talking shop'

Whenever people in an organisation get together socially, and if they are committed and involved individuals, they will tend to 'talk shop'. This means that the work of the organisation, particularly in the area of discussing common problems and keeping each other up-to-date, continues beyond normal office hours. Even if people are present primarily to enjoy themselves, a great deal of useful work may still be done.

'Talking shop' can mean people will look at problems and issues in more detail and will consider more than one possible solution to a problem. They will feel more a part of what goes on at work because they have freely given part of their own time to discussing matters, and ideas may be generated which do not have time to surface and be developed in the hectic hurly-burly of a busy day. On the other hand, much of the talking may be given over to grievances and these may become magnified by such talk. It gives scope for trouble-makers to enlist allies, and it may mean that people become de-motivated because they feel there is little else in their lives other than work.

'Talking shop' is best in those organisations where there is a free and easy attitude to starting times and finishing times as far as work is concerned. They are of least use where there is already a good deal of dissatisfaction and unhappiness with the way things are run.

Attending for the time necessary

This offers a compromise position between attending a meeting and not attending at all. If people are busy, it is useful to accord to them the chance of being present for the part of the meeting that affects them directly. The chairman will have to take a little extra care over the construction of the agenda, but it does mean that people can then both make their contribution to the meeting and get on with some work as well.

Sending a representative

Very often, if a person is in a reasonably senior position and has subordinates who report to him, it may be possible for one of them to attend meetings in his place. If his is not the department or the function which is to be asked for information or comments, and if high-level policy decisions are not to be made, this may be a useful alternative – for the individual – to attending a meeting.

Such delegation frees the individual concerned for other tasks, it gives the representative responsibility and experience which he might otherwise find it difficult to acquire, and it means that the meeting also will benefit by having fewer absentees. However, the subordinate may not have authority to commit his superior on all matters, and this may delay decision-making; the person being represented may become out of touch if he does this too often; and the changing faces of those who attend each time may mean that some of the business has to be repeated because people have not attended previous meetings.

This form of delegation is best in large organisations where a department can have an agreed stance on issues and people can be properly briefed to present this to others. It is at least better to have a substitute present, in most cases, than no one at all. It is least useful where continuity of the committee's activities is important and time must not be wasted in going over old ground unnecessarily.

Reviews of meetings

In addition to all these alternatives to meetings, any organisation should periodically review the meetings it holds. If it finds that a meeting does not appear to serve a useful purpose any longer, then it should be discontinued. There is a tendency for committees once established to stay in being, but surgery is sometimes essential and it may be better for all concerned if this is done rather than to continue wasting people's time and energies when they could be more productively spent.

Since meetings inevitably take people away from their work, it may mean that if meetings do not take place then more work gets done. This work may be of more use to an organisation than spending time looking for things to talk about.

Work is a better alternative to meetings where everybody knows what he or she has to do and can get on with it, where an organisation has more work to do than there is time in which to do it, and where meetings tend to encourage grievances and disruption – if people are busy they will have less time to think up and voice complaints. The problem is that an organisation which is too work- or results-oriented and insufficiently people-oriented may find that a head of steam builds up which eventually bursts out in serious and costly disruption which meetings at an early stage might have defused. It may also be that the quality of work produced deteriorates because, as time goes by, people lose interest, motivation and commitment to the organisation.

Work is preferable to meetings where people have a tendency to meet for the sake of meeting and this needs to be discouraged to some extent. It is least useful if there really are matters of common interest and concern which really do need to be talked through and solutions found or decisions made.

Whatever course of action is adopted, it is always worth exploring the various alternatives before calling a meeting. There will be many occasions when it is simply not possible to do what needs to be done without getting everyone together and making collective decisions. But on those occasions when it is possible to use one of the alternatives described in this chapter, this should lead not only to a general improvement in the effectiveness of the organisation, but also to an increase in the productivity of the meetings which do take place.

15

The Treasurer and Other Officers

The two principal officers in most organisations, the *chairman* and the *secretary*, were considered in Chapters 6 and 7 respectively, but many kinds of meetings have need of other officers. We cannot complete our examination of meetings and committee procedure without considering the parts these other officers play.

The officers that an organisation has should be kept to the necessary minimum. There is no point in having officers for the sake of having officers. However, it is worth bearing in mind that the existence of what are in effect junior officer posts, such as perhaps an *assistant secretary*, a *minutes secretary*, or a *membership secretary*, can provide the opportunity to give experience to those who are being groomed for senior office at some point in the future. This does not have to be the case, but where it is it helps to provide stability, continuity and a steady development as other officers retire and leave.

The treasurer

The main officer an organisation is likely to need in addition to a chairman and a secretary is a treasurer or a finance officer. He is the person who *keeps the financial records*. He needs to take care of the book-keeping, and he prepares budgets, forecasts and any other financial information that an organisation needs. In carrying out this work, he has to remember the need for accuracy and he will need to exercise prudence and probity in framing whatever financial advice he is called upon to give. In many ways he is the conscience of the organisation, a sober and stabilising influence who helps to keep the organisation on the straight and narrow.

In some organisations, especially those which have political objectives or in which most of the members are young and eager to see things happen, the treasurer will need to remind them of the inevitably limited nature of the resources available to them. Money spent on one project or activity cannot be available for another. The treasurer should introduce a note of sound common sense into all discussions which propose the spending of the organisation's money. This becomes especially important in the case of local government, where the finance available is taxpayers' or ratepayers' money.

Not every organisation needs a treasurer or finance officer, but it does if it is handling money. Where products or services have to be costed and sold profitably, there will have to be one. Generally speaking, where there is income and expenditure there will have to be someone who is responsible for supervising and controlling them. Where a great deal of money is involved, as in a large company or a local authority, the treasurer is likely to be a qualified accountant with a whole staff of people to help him to see to every aspect of his work.

However, it is unlikely that a treasurer will be needed if there is no money changing hands or if there is so little that the secretary can take care of it. In small clubs and societies where the only finance to be administered consists of subscriptions, postage and other small items, there may be no need of one. If the organisation is so informal or temporary that an officer structure would be a hindrance rather than an asset, there may be no need for any officers at all, let alone a treasurer.

So, where they exist, treasurers and finance officers need to provide the meetings they attend with relevant, accurate and up-to-date information on past, present and expected economic and financial affairs. They must also interpret this information and advise the other members of the organisation accordingly and appropriately.

When it comes to presenting financial information to non-financial people, there is an overwhelming need for simplicity. Tables of figures may look very attractive to the accountant, but most other people find them simply bewildering. Some means has to be found to permit graphic presentation of financial information. Graphs, charts, histograms can all be used, perhaps with the aid of an overhead projector, to present figures in pictorial form, much as is shown in Figure 16. If these are accompanied by relevant and concise explanations, the treasurer can do a great deal to keep his colleagues properly informed. He can also perform a valuable educational role by encouraging them to progress in their understanding of what figures are able to convey to them and tell them about the state of health of their organisation.

In doing this, it is important to draw attention to key features. It helps also to heighten the impact that illustrations make by a judicious use of colour. The aim should not necessarily be to cover every little detail, but to make sure that people can see and understand 'the bottom line', as it is often called. A treasurer has to ask himself: 'What do they *need* to know?' He must remember that the level of numeracy in our society, like the level of literacy, is not particularly high. He should, therefore, not assume too much about his colleagues' abilities.

When presenting financial information, and indeed any information that is both complex and complicated, the value of visual aids is considerable. In addition to the static aids of the kinds already referred to and illustrated in Figure 16, there are dynamic aids available these days. It is not too difficult for a treasurer with access to video facilities to produce his own reasonably professional moving presentations of financial information. He can also appear on the presentation himself to explain any points which do not speak for themselves. These aids do take time and trouble to prepare, but if they lead to a greater awareness and understanding of financial information in an organisation, they can repay this investment of time and effort many times over. They will also contribute to making the treasurer's job easier over a period of time, because he will have to put less and less effort into trying to get people to understand whatever it is that he is trying to tell them.

There are one or two other guidelines that can be offered which a treasurer can follow in his quest to serve his organisation in the best way possible. He should develop clearly understood and systematic procedures for controlling financial matters and he should always be prepared to try to explain these to those who do not understand them as well as they might. He will remember that people can learn

Fig. 16 Some methods of presenting financial information

Table	1986/7	1987/8	1988/9
Wages and salaries:	24,000.00	26,000.00	28,000.00
Equipment:	15,000.00	17,000.00	19,000.00
Supplies:	9,000.00	11,000.00	13,000.00
Advertising:	2,000.00	2,500.00	3,000.00
Travel:	1,000.00	1,250.00	1,500.00
Miscellaneous:	800.00	900.00	1,000.00

Pie Chart

Histogram

Graph

W&S	Wages & Salaries	A	Advertising
E	Equipment	T	Travel
S	Supplies	M	Miscellaneous

something but then forget it later if they are not in the habit of using the knowledge or skill in the normal course of their everyday lives. So second and even third explanations may be necessary with some people. He will answer questions directly and simply, resisting the temptation to display his financial prowess and blind people with figures. He will report regularly even if he has not been asked for a report. Sometimes, in some organisations, there is an inadequate

Fig. 17   Sample set of accounts for a Parent Teacher Association

INCOME	£.p	EXPENDITURE	£.p
Subscriptions:	45.00	Postage and stationery:	15.75
		Membership cards:	6.24
		Gaming licence and lottery insurance:	5.00
Cheese and wine:	23.67	Cheese and wine:	16.40
Raffle:	158.35	Tickets:	4.23
		Prizes:	10.00
Christmas dance:	149.00	Tickets:	2.75
		Prizes:	5.00
Beetle Drive:	45.85	Prizes:	5.00
Pie and Pea Supper:	70.24	Food:	25.00
Ceilidh:	279.66	Tickets:	12.00
		Prizes:	10.00
		Refreshments:	40.00
Summer Fayre:	1078.41	Posters:	7.50
		Stands:	88.00
		Refreshments:	102.89
Grand Draw:	279.60	Tickets:	11.90
		Prizes:	10.00
Cookery demonstration:	17.50	Food:	12.58
Donations:	286.22	Speakers' Expenses:	50.80
Cash in hand	17.83	Trophies:	85.44
Reserves	183.00	School equipment:	
		Video:	389.00
		Copier:	895.00
		Computer:	573.85
		Library:	250.00
Total:	2634.33		2634.33

recognition of importance of financial matters and in such cases it is the treasurer's job to remind them. Regular reports, even if short, make the point, which will sink in eventually. Ideally, he should also train someone to take over when he leaves or in case he is temporarily incapacitated by illness or some other cause. In money matters, as in many others, continuity is important. This extends also to the way in which financial records are maintained – as a general rule, the form of presentation should not be changed without good reason.

Looking at the treasurer's job from another standpoint, how can an organisation get the most out of its financial adviser and his expertise? People should not be afraid to ask questions, even if they feel that by doing so they may appear a little foolish. A good treasurer will establish a climate in which embarrassment does not occur. Expect to be shown records and ask for explanations. Look for value for money in activities. Insist on simplicity in presentation. Check figures. In these and other ways, you can ensure that the organisation gets the best out of its treasurer and that the treasurer gets the best out of his organisation. The benefits are mutual.

The vice-chairman

It is quite possible that for the whole of his year of office a vice-chairman may have nothing whatsoever to do. This is because the vice-chairman has no duties as such, other than to take the chair in the absence of the chairman. So his may seem to be a kind of non-job which is best given to someone who only wants a position and does not expect to do any work.

It needs to be remembered, however, that the vice-chairman may have to take over from the chairman and, since this is the key job, at least during meetings, some care should be exercised in selecting him. He may need training and, if this is the case, it is best done early rather than late. It also helps if the chairman is the kind of person who does not insist on chairing every meeting, but stays away occasionally so that the vice-chairman can take over. If he starts with meetings which are easy and routine, he can gradually introduce the vice-chairman to more difficult meetings. In some organisations, it may even be worth having two vice-chairmen. In this way, if one of them proves incapable of performing the chairman's duties the other one can slot in without the embarrassment of resignation and the election of a replacement before the next annual general meeting.

Some organisations overcome the apparent irrelevance of having a vice-chairman by giving him a job to do. This is often the post of being the organisation's press and public relations officer. This has the merit of ensuring that the vice-chairmanship is not a sinecure and it does give him a potentially important job to do.

The minutes secretary

Sometimes, where the secretary's duties are wide-ranging and he needs to play an active part in meetings, it can be difficult for him to take in enough of what is going on in the meeting to be able to write good minutes. It is virtually impossible to write notes for minutes and play an active part in the discussions at the same time: you can only do one or the other. If someone can be found who is willing to take over the responsibility for the minutes, this can be a consider-able asset to both the secretary and the meeting as a whole. Sometimes this fact is rewarded by calling the minutes secretary the *assistant secretary*. A small price to pay for greater efficiency.

Membership secretary

Another of the secretary's functions which can usefully be hived off, perhaps to a young and enthusiastic individual, is that of the recruitment of new members. In many clubs and societies this is a vital activity. For instance, in Round Table the members have to retire at the age of forty. This means that a steady stream of suitable new members is necessary.

So a membership secretary can help to boost membership, keep membership records and keep the organisation in touch with past members or those who have moved away or who may be in hospital, and collect the annual subscriptions.

Public relations officer

If the vice-chairman is not the PRO, it can be worthwhile electing someone to the post. Clearly, they will need communication skills of a high order. They can be given the task of telling the world – through local press, local radio and perhaps regional television – of the organisation's activities. This helps to recruit new members, to provide public recognition for members' achievements and generally to improve the image of the organisation locally.

Other officers

There are several other officers which organisations of various kinds may feel they require. A *speakers' officer* is useful in those organisations which like to combine business at a meeting with listening to someone who has (hopefully) something worthwhile to say in an interesting and lively way. More formal meetings, especially in local authorities, will find that among the officers present there is the *solicitor*, or the *architect*, or the *engineer*. The more complex the organisation's activities, the more wide-ranging will be the numbers and functions of the officers it will be necessary to have present.

Nevertheless, an organisation should not be encouraged to have superfluous officers. It should have only those which it needs to conduct its business. No one wants to create a situation in which there are more chiefs than indians. That is not going to help any organisation to improve the efficiency and effectiveness of its operations.

16

Committee Language

Ab initio   From the beginning. [There are many Latin terms used in meetings, though their use is not now as widespread as it once was.]

Abstention   When a person abstains he neither votes for the motion nor against it. Abstentions are often recorded, as well as votes.

Acclamation, vote by   A method by which a meeting shows its decision by clapping and cheering.

Addendum   An amendment which adds words.

Addressing the chair   The convention is that when you speak in meetings you always speak as if to the chairman only.

Ad hoc   For a particular purpose. An ad hoc committee meets for a set purpose and then is disbanded.

Ad infinitum   Indefinitely.

Adjournment   A meeting stops and does not resume its business until a later time or date.

Admission of press (and public)   The press (and the public) now have right of admission to many local authority committee and sub-committee meetings. If they are excluded, the reason must be clearly stated (e.g. an application for a loan has been made by a local industrialist and the details are commercially confidential).

Agenda   The list of items of business which a meeting is to discuss.

Amended motion   The original motion with amendments incorporated to produce a new text.

Amendment   A proposal to change the wording of a motion.

Amendment, amendment to   A proposal to change an amendment.

Amendment, counter   A substitute for the original motion.

Amendment, notice of   An indication to the chairman of a wish to propose a further amendment when the present one has been decided.

AGM   Annual General Meeting.

Annual Report and Accounts   A financial statement which many organisations must produce every year.

A posteriori   From the effect to the cause (a form of reasoning).

A priori   From the cause to the effect (a form of reasoning).

Appendix   Supplementary matter at the end of a report.

Articles of Association   The internal regulations of how a company is run.

Auditors   Nominated people who check the authenticity of an organisation's accounts every year. With formal organisations they are usually professionally qualified in accountancy.

Ballot   Voting by recording on paper so that the vote is secret. Usually the votes are placed in a sealed box.

Block vote   A system used by the Trades Union Congress in which a union has votes according to the size of its membership and casts them as a block.

Bona fide   In good faith.

Candidate   A person who has been nominated or who has put himself forward for election to office.

Card vote   See *Block vote*. It is sometimes called card vote because those voting have cards with the number of votes printed on.

Casting vote   A second vote which a chairman has and can only use when a vote is tied with equal numbers voting for and against.

Catching chairman's eye   Attracting the chairman's attention so that he asks you to speak.

Caucus meeting   Meeting of a party group on a council or of likeminded members of an organisation, usually to agree a common approach to matters.

Closure   The termination of discussion in order to proceed to a vote.

Committee   A body consisting of a specific number of people set up to discuss, decide and report on matters referred to it by its parent body.

Composite motion   One motion formed by combining elements from other similar motions.

Constitution   The rules governing the structure and functions of an organisation.

Convenor   One who organises or calls a meeting.

Co-opting, co-option   The procedure of adding people to a committee at the invitation of the members of the committee rather than the parent body.

Correspondence   Letters received by a secretary which he then reads out to the meeting for the members to decide what to do about them.

Data   Items of information or facts on which a report going to committee can be based.

De facto   Actually existing, though this is not usually because of a legal right to do so.

De jure   By right, though this does not guarantee that something will be actually existing.

Delegate   A person who has been sent to a meeting to represent a group of people, organisation or some other body.

Deputation   A small group of people sent to put a case on behalf of a larger group of people.

Division   Separating into groups in order to vote.

Ejection from a meeting   Being asked to leave or removed bodily.

Election   Choosing by voting.

Emergency motion   One decided immediately without any deferment to the next meeting as may be usual.

En bloc   All together

Executive committee   A smaller group than the parent body, charged with the responsibility for managing an organisation's affairs between general meetings.

Ex officio   By virtue of the office held. Secretaries are often members of committees 'ex officio'.

Exhaustive ballot   A method of voting for several candidates whereby the one with the lowest vote each time drops out, until the winner has a majority of the total possible votes.

EGM   Extraordinary General Meeting.

Filibuster   Speaking until there is no time left in which a decision can be taken.

Gagging   Preventing a person from speaking by using procedural devices to limit the opportunities for members to speak.

Getting the floor   Receiving the chairman's permission to speak.

Group meeting See *Caucus meeting.*

'Guillotine' closure Closing a debate by a pre-set time, whether or not every aspect of the subject has been considered.

Heckling Calling out when someone is speaking, in an attempt to put them off their stride, or otherwise disrupting proceedings.

In camera With no members of the press or public present; in private; in secret.

'Kangaroo' closure A method of limiting debate used in Parliament by which the Speaker selects those amendments that will be debated.

Main question The chief subject under discussion.

Male fide In bad faith.

Mandate The authority to carry out a programme, conferred by having been supported explicity or implicity by the way the people affected have voted.

Minutes A written record of the proceedings of a meeting, by agenda items, which records the decisions made.

Modus operandi Way or method of working.

Motion A proposal put to a meeting to act in a certain way or to offer an opinion upon a subject and which is conventionally expressed in a positive rather than a negative way.

Mutatis mutandis With the necessary changes being made.

Naming a member of a meeting If a chairman 'names' (i.e. speaks the name) after warning a person for his behaviour, the person must then leave the meeting and take no further part in it.

Negative motions Motions which propose *not* to do something.

Nemine contradicente (nem con) With no one speaking against.

Nemine dissentiente (nem dis) With no one dissenting. (Votes are only unanimous when everyone present actually votes for them and does not abstain from voting.)

Next business A proposed move to the next item, leaving the present one unresolved.

Nomination Putting someone's name forward as a candidate for office.

Notice of meeting A letter stating the date, time, venue and business for a meeting.

Notice of motion A motion set out for discussion at the next, rather than the current, meeting.

Officers Those with special functions in an organisation.

Order, preservation of Making sure a meeting is quiet enough and orderly enough for business to be done.

Ordinary business The normal matters on which the members of an organisation meet together to make decisions.

Pious motion A motion which merely gives an opinion.

Point of explanation An explanation by a member of a meeting of some questioned behaviour.

Point of information The offering of information, made via the chair, to a speaker during his speech.

Point of order A challenge to the way a meeting is being conducted.

Precedent An earlier decision by a body which prescribes future behaviour, in effect.

Premise The statement on which an argument is based.

Previous question See *Next business*.

Privilege (and qualified privilege) Freedom from suit for libel or slander (e.g. in parliamentary business).

Procedural motion One concerned with how a meeting is being run.

Proposer of motion The first person to speak on a motion.

Proxy Someone who votes in someone else's place, with their agreement.

Quorum The minimum number of people who must be present for a meeting to take place.

Reference back Sending a report or proposal back to the body from which it came, usually as a rejection or for further consideration.

Remit (usually to executive committee) To forward a proposal for a committee to decide.

Report of meeting An account of a meeting which does not necessarily follow agenda order and thus is distinct from the minutes.

Rescind (a resolution) To withdraw or cancel a decision made by motion at an earlier meeting.

Resolution A motion becomes a resolution when it has been voted on and agreed.

Rider A statement added to another to make it clearer.

Right of reply The right of a proposer to reply at the end of a debate to points made by others.

Rostrum The platform at a conference or large meeting on which people stand to speak.

Rules of debate The conventions according to which meetings are conducted and which derive from parliamentary procedures.

Scrutineer One who totals the votes in a ballot.

Seconder (of motion) One who speaks second in favour of a nomination or motion.

Show of hands Raising one hand in the air to vote.

Sine die Without a date being set.

Special meeting One called for a specified purpose in addition to ordinary meetings.

Standing orders The rules by which a meeting is conducted (see Fig. 18 on page 166).

Status quo Things remaining unaltered.

Sub-committee A smaller group which reports to a committee.

Sub judice Under consideration.

Sub rosa In secret; privately.

Substantive motion An amended motion when it has been carried.

Suspension of member Prohibiting a member from attending meetings.

Suspension of standing orders Moved in order to allow proceedings which standing orders preclude.

Tellers Those appointed to count votes.

Terms of reference The limits of the scope of business.

Ultra vires Beyond a body's legal powers.

Unanimously carried With everybody present voting for a proposal.

Verbatim Word for word.

Veto The power of a person or body to prevent a proposal being acted upon.

Voting procedures The methods by which votes are taken.

Withdrawal of motion This can usually only be done with the consent of the meeting, for a motion once proposed becomes the property of the meeting.

Fig. 18   An example of Standing Orders

Standing Orders

At the first meeting held in the Meeting Rooms on Saturday, 14 April 198— the Standing Orders as follows were accepted:

1 Meetings
(a) Ordinary meetings shall be held at an agreed time after the publication of the agenda. The Annual Meeting for the election of officers, etc., shall be held, on a date to be determined.
(b) For the purposes of maintaining contact between the Executive and the General Committee, five representatives of the latter may attend meetings in a consultative capacity and without voting power, provided that the number of such representatives shall not exceed one-third of the membership.

2 Officers
The following officers shall be appointed at the Annual Meeting:

(a) Chairman
(b) Vice-Chairman
(c) Secretary
(d) Treasurer

The functions of a Secretary shall include the convening of meetings and the preparation of the agenda.

3 Executive Committee
The officers, together with two other members to be appointed at the Annual Meeting, shall constitute the Executive Committee.

4 Casual Vacancies
Casual vacancies among the officers or in the Executive Committee shall be filled at an ordinary or other meeting of which appropriate notice shall be given.

5 Rules of Debate
(a) The proposer of a motion or of an amendment shall be allowed ten minutes for his speech. No extension of time shall be allowed.
(b) Each succeeding speaker shall be allowed five minutes. No extension of time shall be allowed.
(c) Whenever an amendment is made upon any motion, no second amendment shall be taken into consideration until the first amendment is disposed of. If that amendment be carried, it shall then be put as a substantive motion, upon which a further amendment may be moved. If the first amendment be negatived then a further amendment may be moved to the original ques-

tion: but only one amendment shall be submitted for discussion at one time. 'The Previous Question' is for all purposes of order dealt with as an amendment except that it shall have precedence over all other amendments.

(*d*) The decision of the chairman on any point shall be final. If any decision be questioned, it must be done at the next meeting.

(*e*) The mover of an original motion shall have, in addition to the general privileges of debate, the right of reply upon the original motion or upon one amendment, and the mover of an amendment which has become the substantive motion shall have a similar right of reply. The right of reply shall be exercised only after the closure has been applied and subsequently no further debate shall be allowed on the same question. No member shall speak more than once on the same motion or amendment except in the exercise of the right of reply and no new matter shall be introduced by the mover in reply.

(*f*) Any debate, except that on the main question, may be closed by a motion 'That the question be now put' being moved, seconded, and carried, such motion to be put to the meeting without debate: but no speech shall be interrupted for the purpose of proposing such a motion. Where an amendment is under discussion the motion shall apply only to that amendment. After the question has been put on any amendment, a motion 'That the main question be now considered' can be moved, seconded and put to the meeting without debate. The chairman shall then decide whether the debate on the main question is necessary and when the time has come when the main question may be fairly put.

(*g*) When the chairman rises to speak, members shall immediately take their seats. Any member who shall wilfully disregard the ruling of the chairman after due warning, or shall be guilty of gross disorderly conduct in interrupting the proceedings, shall be immediately suspended from further attendance at meetings and shall have his or her conduct dealt with by the officers.

(*h*) Every motion shall be put to the vote by a show of hands unless otherwise decided by a majority of the members present.

(*i*) All elections shall be by secret and exhaustive ballot. The candidate with the lowest number of votes to be eliminated from each ballot. Where the total votes cast in favour of the two candidates with the lowest votes does not exceed the number of votes cast in favour of the candidate with the third lowest number of votes, the last two candidates to be eliminated from the ballot.

(*j*) Where two or more like vacancies are to be filled, members shall vote for the total number of vacancies at each ballot. Any ballot paper having less than the required number of votes shall be declared void.

17

Checklist for Effective Meetings

This final chapter presents for easy reference a list of the essential points to observe in order to conduct, and to participate in, effective meetings. They are organised according to the chapter-order of the book, so that you can easily refer back to the appropriate pages for a more detailed exposition of the point being made. In the vast majority of cases the points have been made explicitly earlier, but in some they are inferred from what has been said already.

Purposes and Preconditions (Chapter 2)
1   Ask yourself: Is a meeting really necessary? (see also Chapter 14).
2   Make sure that a meeting has a clear purpose.
3   Consider at an early stage, in general terms, what the agenda should contain.
4   Make the size of the meeting as small as is reasonably possible.
5   Ask only those people who are necessary for a successful meeting to attend.
6   Make sure the venue is an appropriate one.
7   Allow a reasonable amount of time for a meeting.
8   Consider at an early stage who would be the best chairman for the meeting (where there is a choice).
9   Consider at an early stage what form the minutes should eventually take.
10   Make all the *necessary* arrangements for the meeting.

Action Before a Meeting (Chapter 3)

1 Define objectives as clearly as possible.
2 Identify which are the key agenda items.
3 Plan your approach to the meeting carefully.
4 Have a 'Plan B' ready in case the first plan proves in-appropriate.
5 Brief yourself properly on the items to be considered at the meeting.
6 Learn to read efficiently the papers for meetings.
7 Make your own notes on the content of each item (self-recitation).
8 Follow a study strategy for really important items.
9 Research a subject if necessary to improve your understanding of it.
10 Consider lobbying other members of meeting for support for your point of view.

How a Meeting Proceeds (Chapter 4)

1 Study the openings of meetings as much may be learned from this.
2 Study how meetings work through their agendas.
3 Ensure that the order of items is the most appropriate one.
4 Ensure that there is a quorum of the members present.
5 Frame motions positively.
6 Frame amendments carefully and concisely.
7 Ensure that decisions are clear to you.
8 Follow the appropriate 'rules of debate'.
9 Only use points of order to query or challenge procedure and not to make speeches.
10 Use other procedural motions sparingly and with great care.
11 Study the closings of meetings as much may be learned from this as well.

How to Participate in a Meeting (Chapter 5)

1 Find out what has happened at similar meetings in the past.
2 Find out who will also be present at the meeting.
3 Be ready to make a contribution.
4 Contribute early.
5 Make speaking notes to base your contribution on.

6   Seek to build on common ground to avoid unnecessarily losing allies.
7   Practise beforehand.
8   Be sensitive to body language, your own and others, especially in areas of:

   (*a*)   eye contact
   (*b*)   facial expressions
   (*c*)   head movements
   (*d*)   gestures and body movements
   (*e*)   posture and stance
   (*f*)   proximity and orientation
   (*g*)   bodily contact (if any)
   (*h*)   appearance and physique
   (*i*)   timing and synchronisation
   (*j*)   nonverbal aspects of speech.

The Chair (Chapter 6)

1   Know the basic functions and duties of the chairman.
2   Have the right personal qualities.
3   Have an appropriate style of chairmanship.
4   Control the 'hidden agenda'.
5   Control disruption effectively.
6   Try to reduce the role of the chairman to involve the others present more.
7   Ensure that the meeting reaches the decisions that it needs to.
8   Try to be a 'perfect' chairman (see list on page 67).

The Secretary (Chapter 7)

1   Know the basic functions and duties of the secretary.
2   Have the right personal qualities.
3   Be organised.
4   Construct the agenda in consultation with the chairman.
5   Seek to influence the chairman so that you both have a common approach to the organisation and the matters under discussion.
6   Remember the other roles of the secretary.
7   Complete all secretarial tasks on time.
8   Pay particular attention to pre-meeting tasks.
9   Make sure that all post-meeting tasks are completed.
10   Study the law of meetings (see Further Reading).

Writing the Minutes (Chapter 8)

1 Ensure that the minutes record all the essential details of what happened.
2 Prepare an over-all structure for the minutes in advance, based upon the agenda.
3 Concentrate on recording decisions.
4 Keep to the order of items as given on the agenda.
5 Make more notes of what happens and is said during the meeting than you will need for the minutes.
6 Write in a formal and impersonal style.
7 Write in the past tense.
8 Aim for conciseness.
9 For important meetings, where it is necessary to be sure of getting everything right have more than one person taking the minutes.
10 Consider when minutes are not necessary and when a report of the meeting might be more suitable.

Action After a Meeting (Chapter 9)

1 Have a checklist of things to do.
2 Inform others who need to know what happened at the meeting.
3 Foster good public relations.
4 Have a good personal filing system.
5 Write the necessary memos and letters.
6 Prepare for the next meeting (this applies not just to the secretary but to everyone who attends a meeting).

Problems with Meetings (Chapter 11)

1 Avoid becoming entangled in procedure.
2 Avoid too many amendments (and in any case, see the chairman takes them one at a time).
3 Avoid too many points of order.
4 Avoid confusion over what decisions have been taken.
5 Avoid disruptive behaviour.
6 Avoid uncertain openings and closings.
7 Make sure decisions *are* made where appropriate or necessary.
8 Avoid badly run meetings.
9 Make sure meetings start on time where you can.

10 Avoid wandering from the point.
11 Avoid 'hidden objectives'.
12 Do what you can (if the chairman does not) to encourage everyone present to participate in the meeting.
13 Avoid unnecessary conflict.
14 Avoid consensus and compromise where these will not be productive.
15 Replace a weak chairman if you can.
16 Avoid making meetings longer than they need be.
17 Make sure the right people attend a meeting.
18 Avoid too many meetings.
19 Ensure that a quorum will be present.
20 Encourage all those attending to prepare properly for the meeting.
21 Reduce the paperwork required for a meeting as far as you can.

Analysing Meetings (Chapter 12)

1 Analyse content.
2 Analyse intentions.
3 Analyse treatment.
4 Analyse evaluation.

In particular:

5 Analyse preparation.
6 Analyse the achievement of objectives.
7 Analyse the sequence of items.
8 Analyse how the agenda items are dealt with.
9 Analyse the clarity of the decisions which are made.
10 Analyse the participation in the proceedings by all those present and the contribution rate.
11 Analyse the action taken after the meeting has finished.
12 Analyse the over-all effect and success of the meeting and identify causes of failure and suggest remedies.

Preparing and Presenting Reports to Meetings (Chapter 13)

1 Follow the techniques of effective writing.
2 Use a report-writing strategy:

(*a*) Prepare
(*b*) Assess

(c) Plan
(d) Express
(e) Review

3 Use a report-presenting strategy:

   (a) Introduction
   (b) Body
   (c) Conclusion

4 Speak from notes.
5 Speak clearly.
6 Use statistics sparingly.
7 Use body language sensitively.
8 Talk *to* not *at* the audience.
9 Aim for accuracy, conciseness, clarity and simplicity.
10 Rehearse before presenting your report (use video-recording facilities if you can).

Alternatives to Meetings (Chapter 14)

Explore the possibilities of:

1 Delegating.
2 Telephone calls.
3 Teleconferencing.
4 The 'nil return'.
5 Computer access for information.
6 One-man bands (where appropriate).
7 Seeing people personally.
8 Newsletters.
9 Memos.
10 Videos.
11 'Talking shop'.
12 Working instead of meeting.
13 Sending a representative instead of attending yourself.
14 Reviewing (at regular intervals) the meetings that are held, to see if they are still relevant.
15 Attending meetings only for the time necessary to make your contribution.

And finally, two additional points which may be useful:

Understand committee and meetings language (see Chapter 16).
Know and understand your organisation's Standing Orders (see Chapter 16).

Further Reading

Banks, R. A. (1983) *Living English*, Hodder & Stoughton.

Bentley, C. F. (1970) *Handbook for Chairmen and Secretaries*, A. H. & A. W. Reed.

Campion, Sir G., *Introduction to the Procedure of the House of Commons*, Macmillan.

Castle, D. & Wade, J. (1980) *Public Speaking*, Teach Yourself Books, Hodder & Stoughton.

Citrine, Lord (1952) *ABC of Chairmanship*, N.C.L.C.

Compton, H. (1962) *Conveying Ideas*, Cleaver-Hume.

De Leeuw, M. & E. (1965) *Read Better, Read Faster*, Pelican.

Eyre, E. C. (1979) *Effective Communication Made Simple*, Heinemann.

Gondin, W. R. & Mammen, E. W. (1980) *The Art of Speaking Made Simple*, Heinemann.

Hall, L. (1977, 2nd edn) *Meetings: Their Law and Practice*, Macdonald & Evans.

Harding Boulton, A. (1977, 6th edn) *Shackleton on the Law and Practice of Meetings*, Sweet & Maxwell.

Harlow, E. & Compton, H. (1967) *Practical Communication*, Longman.

Harrison, R. (1974) *Beyond Words*, Prentice-Hall.

James, D. (1979) *Letter-writing*, Teach Yourself Books, Hodder & Stoughton.

Lloyd, H. & Lloyd, P. (1984) *Public Relations*, Teach Yourself Books, Hodder & Stoughton.

Mackenzie, R. A. (1972) *The Time Trap*, McGraw-Hill.

Maude, B. (1974) *Practical Communication for Managers*, Longman.

May, Sir T. E., *Parliamentary Practice*, Butterworth.

Mitchell, J. (1974) *How to Write Reports*, Fontana.

Morris, D. (1977) *Manwatching*, Cape.

Palgrave, Sir R. (1964) *Chairman's Handbook*, Dent.

Phythian, B. A. (1985) *Good English*, Teach Yourself Books, Hodder & Stoughton.

Piper, A. G. (1984) *Book-keeping*, Teach Yourself Books, Hodder & Stoughton.

Pitfield, R. R. & Hughes, P. F. (1979) *The Law and Procedure of Meetings*, Secretaries Journal Ltd.

Ransom, M., *Chairman's and Debator's Handbook*, Routledge & Kegan Paul.

Shackleton, F. (ed) (1956) *Chairman's Guide and Secretary's Companion*, Ward Lock.

Shaw, Sir S. & Smith, Judge D. (1974, 4th edn) *The Law of Meetings*, Macdonald & Evans.

Taylor, H. M. & Mears, A. G. (1983, 10th edn) *The Right Way to Conduct Meetings, Conferences and Discussions*, Elliot.

Turk, C. & Kirkman, J. (1982) *Effective Writing*, Spon.

Wainwright, G. R. (1968) *Towards Efficiency in Reading*, Cambridge University Press.

Wainwright, G. R. (1972) *Rapid Reading Made Simple*, Heinemann.

Wainwright, G. R. (1979) *People and Communication*, Macdonald & Evans.

Wainwright, G. R. (1984) *Report Writing*, Management Update.

Wainwright, G. R. (1984) *People and Communication Workbook*, Macdonald & Evans.

Wainwright, G. R. (1985) *Body Language*, Teach Yourself Books, Hodder & Stoughton.

Index

BODY LANGUAGE

GORDON R. WAINWRIGHT

We all use body language. This practical guide will train you to use and interpret it more effectively: to reinforce what you say and do, and to recognise what others are seeking to conceal.

Over ninety per cent of all face-to-face communication is nonverbal, and the silent messages of body language – gestures, eye and head movement, posture, facial expression, proximity and bodily contact – often reveal more than the spoken word in conveying true feelings or attitudes and signalling confidence, aggression, boredom or attraction. These messages are particularly significant in influencing first impressions and the self-image we project to others.

This book explains the different aspects of body language and provides a wide range of observational and practical exercises that will enhance your perception and understanding of nonverbal communication – in everyday encounters, in personal relationships and in interviews and meetings at work. The emphasis throughout is on developing your own body language skills: to contribute to personal growth and self-development, and to improve your effectiveness in face-to-face communication generally.

TEACH YOURSELF BOOKS

GOOD ENGLISH

B. A. PHYTHIAN

This practical guide and reference handbook will help you improve your own use of English in everyday life and enhance your appreciation of good English writing.

The book first provides handy summaries of the main rules of grammar and punctuation. It then examines some of the more common errors in spoken and written English, before giving practical advice on spelling and helpful definitions of words which are frequently confused and misused.

The second half of the book focuses on the correct and effective use of English in a wide variety of contexts, and illustrates the different types of language and style which contribute to the subtlety and variety of English expression. A particularly useful feature of the book is an extensive guide to the conventions of written English in everyday life, including business and commercial English, letters, reports, summaries and precis.

TEACH YOURSELF BOOKS

LETTER WRITING

DAVID JAMES

A complete guide to writing letters which say exactly what you want to say – and bring the desired response.

This book explains how to write effective letters. David James offers practical advice on the choice of layout, style and 'tone', and then examines different kinds of letters ranging from the simple thank-you note to the more involved job application or sales letter to a potential customer.

Numerous sample letters illustrate correct forms and common errors, and highlight the various conventions and courtesies observed in different parts of the world. Forms of address and a list of common abbreviations are also included for easy reference, making this a book for every home or office.

TEACH YOURSELF BOOKS